Local area networks

An introduction to the technology

Local area networks

An introduction to the technology

John E. McNamara

digital DIGITAL PRESS

Design by Richard C. Bartlett
Illustrations by Carol Keller
Cover design by Paul Souza, WGBH Design

Printed in the United States of America

10   9   8   7   6

Order number EY-00051-DP
ISBN 0-932376-79-7

Teflon is a trademark of DuPont de Nemours Company Inc.

Library of Congress Cataloging in Publication Data

McNamara, John E.
    Local area networks.

    Includes bibliographies and index.
    1. Local area networks (Computer networks) I. Title.
TK5105.7.M36   1985   001.64′404   84-26013
ISBN 0-932376-79-7

Contents

Preface

This book is intended for students, computer system managers, tele-communications managers, and others who want to become more familiar with local area networks. Since product offerings in this area are constantly changing, a deliberate attempt has been made to emphasize the general principles, operating characteristics, and problem areas of local area network hardware and software, rather than cite specific product examples.

This book is also designed to give people who are thinking of buying a local area network familiarity with the concepts involved. Here again, the aim is not to survey current product offerings, but rather to assist the reader in making an intelligent choice and asking appropriate questions of prospective vendors.

The book begins with a general introduction, discussing the development of local area networks and emphasizing their possible uses. This is followed by more detailed treatment of physical factors: topology, media, and installation requirements. Next, the hardware that permits programs to access the local area network and transfer data is discussed. Then, software is covered, starting with an introduction to communications protocols. Finally, the combined base of hardware and software knowledge from the previous parts of the book are used in discussions of network services, network expansion, and the problems associated with creating large networks. The need for standards is implied throughout the book, and a brief final chapter discusses the creation of standards and their current status.

Acknowledgment

First and foremost, I would like to thank Larry Allen, of MIT's Laboratory for Computer Science. It was he who suggested that I write the book, he who answered many of my questions, and he who provided enthusiasm and support to propel me through the dry spells.

Second, a special note of thanks to the reviewers and to the people I interviewed during the writing process. From Proteon Incorporated, these include Al Marshall, John Shriver, and especially Howard Salwen. Digital Equipment Corporation contributors included Tom Ermolovich, Tony Lauck, Dave Mitton, and Rich Seifert. At 3Com Corporation, Dr.

Robert Metcalfe, one of the creators of Ethernet, made several contributions. At MIT's Laboratory for Computer Science, Dr. David D. Clark, author of several important papers in the field, was very helpful. In addition to these individuals, there were several reviewers whose identities were never known to me, but they certainly deserve my thanks. I would also like to note that the views expressed in the book are my own and probably do not agree exactly with any of the contributors, since many had radically divergent views.

Last, but by no means least, the personnel of Digital Press have been of invaluable assistance. Under the conscientious guidance of Lucy Chen, they have worked their miracles of editing, typesetting, art work, layout, graphic design, and countless other tasks with pride and talent that makes working with them a wonderful partnership.

January 1985   John E. McNamara

Local area networks

An introduction to the technology

1 Introduction

Networks are a familiar concept because radio, television, railway, and highway networks have been with us for decades. An additional form of network, the computer network, has also been around for more than twenty years, but is less familiar. Computer networks have been less noticeable than other forms of network because we do not see the network itself; rather, we see the results of using the network when we make travel reservations and perform financial transactions.

Computer networks provide many services besides travel reservations and financial transactions, but these applications show two important features of computer networks:

1. They provide shared access to information, such as airline flight status or account balances.
2. They permit the movement of data, such as flight status updates or financial transfers.

Until recently, these features have been most important to geographically dispersed businesses, so computer networks have spanned wide geographic areas—a state or an entire country. However, within the past few years a new form of computer network, the "local area network," has become important. Local area networks are data communications systems that span a physically limited area (generally less than a mile or two); provide high bandwidth communication (using a frequency range of several megaHertz) over inexpensive media (generally coaxial cable or twisted pair); provide a switching capability (the ability for users to selectively connect to each other); and are usually owned by the user (i.e., not provided by a common carrier or similar company licensed to provide the service).

Three of the physical attributes—limited area, high bandwidth, and user ownership—make local area networks substantially different from existing computer networks. Existing computer networks operate over the international telephone network, where distances are great, bandwidth is generally narrow, and ownership is vested in licensed common carriers or government agencies. Despite these differences, many of the problems faced by the two types of networks are similar: the network must be planned in advance, facilities must be purchased and installed, and traffic must be estimated before installation and monitored after installation. In addition, for both conventional and local area networks, no single architecture, transmission medium, or switching technique is appropriate for all applications.

In addition to the physical differences between conventional computer networks and local area networks, there is an important difference in application. Both types of network permit users to have shared access to data bases, but local area networks go a step further and allow users to have shared access to many common hardware/software resources such as storage, input/output, and communication devices. The concept of shared access to resources is the most important element of local area networks and is discussed later in greater detail.

To understand how local area networks became such an important part of computing, it is necessary to review the history and evolution of previous computing systems with particular emphasis on the shortcomings that led to the development of local area networks.

Most computation in the past twenty years has been accomplished on timesharing systems and batch systems. The basic concept of timesharing is to divide a large computer's time into very brief periods; during each period, a single user has complete control of the machine. This concept allows users to write programs, run them, and debug them from a "terminal." In contrast, batch systems require users to punch cards, submit the card deck to an operator, and wait several hours to learn whether the program has succeeded. Timesharing systems have been very successful for applications requiring frequent human interaction because they save people a lot of time and are much less frustrating than batch systems. Batch systems remain dominant in applications where large amounts of data are processed with minimal human intervention.

Timesharing systems have been so successful that the number of users on typical systems often grows to the point that the systems' response times during periods of peak load become annoyingly slow. Although some users can respond to this problem by changing their work hours to avoid the busiest periods, the only viable long-term solution is to purchase more computing power.

Purchasing more computer power can be accomplished either by increasing the capacity of the central computing facility or by placing more computing capability directly in the hands of the user.

Increasing the capacity of the central computing facility is not always easy to do. In some cases, the manufacturer of the timesharing system currently in use does not have a larger model, and a change of vendors is required. When a change of vendors means a change of software, the switchover is traumatic for most users. In other cases, the next model has far more capability and cost than is desirable. A possible solution to this problem is to buy a second computer of the same size and manufacturer. Half of the users are then connected to one computer and half to the other. Problems then arise when capacity is available on one computer, but prospective users cannot use the capacity because their files are on the other (overloaded) computer. If only both computers could access the same files . . .

A simple network for achieving access to files from two computers is shown in Figure 1, but it has two major difficulties. One difficulty is that each computer spends some portion of its time transferring files to the other computer to serve those users who have logged on to the

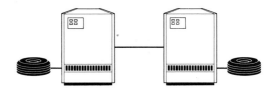

Figure 1. Two computers sharing file access

computer that doesn't have their files. The second, and quite serious, difficulty is that the figure does not generalize well to multiple computers. Figure 2, Figure 3, or a combination thereof is required.

In Figure 2, the cost of the communication interfaces and, in some cases, the cost of communication lines is very high and increases dramatically each time a computer is added to the network. In Figure 3, the communication interface cost and line cost are low, but each computer spends some amount of time transferring data for the other computers rather than performing computational tasks for its users. In addition, the linear arrangement of computers and communications links is very unreliable; failure of a single computer or communications link splits the network into two parts that cannot communicate.

The preceding paragraphs have outlined the problems associated with increasing the capacity of a central computing facility. That was only one of two alternatives mentioned for obtaining more computational power. The second alternative was to place more computational capability directly in the hands of the user, that is, to increase the capability at the user's terminal.

The computational capability available in user terminals has risen greatly in the past decade, primarily because of technology changes in terminal manufacture. With the advent of extremely inexpensive microprocessors, many of the complex circuits used in terminals can be

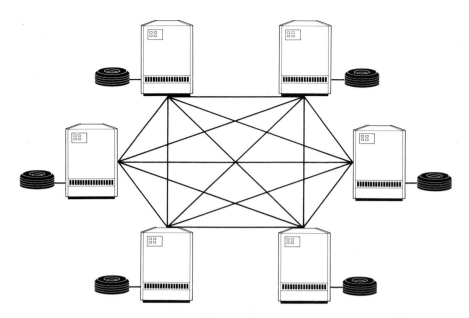

Figure 2. Multinode mesh network

more easily and cheaply implemented using microprocessors. Once a terminal has a microprocessor built in, the conversion of that terminal to a small computer is a short step away. The addition of sufficient memory can be readily accomplished with modern low-cost memory chips; a Winchester disk can provide low-cost mass storage; and a low-cost printer can provide hardcopy.

Once user terminals have become personal computers with mass storage, the data transmission requirements change from the slow speeds necessary for transmitting keyboard input and screen updates to the high speeds necessary for transferring files. Furthermore, the transmission and reception are no longer just to the associated "host computer," but rather to any of several computers. A real computer network like Figure 2 or Figure 3 is needed, but a better design is needed because of the large number of points being connected. Some of the designs for local area networks that will solve the problem of connecting a large number of points are discussed in Chapters 2 and 3.

Creating networks of personal computers is not just an expanded case of linking large computers, however. For economic and other reasons, some services that were provided on each machine in a network of large timesharing systems should be shared among the users of a personal computer network. Examples of the network services that should be shared include access to file services, printer services, and

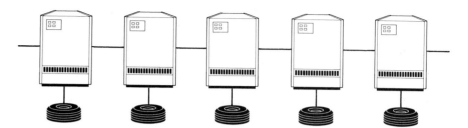

Figure 3. Linear network

communication services. Although the concept of network services ("servers") will be developed more fully later, let us explore here a few motivations for having network services.

The need for network file services and network printer services comes from the logistics problems associated with disks and printers. Disks may crash; thus they should be periodically copied ("backed up"). As users of personal computers and word processors know, one eventually gains enough confidence in the disks that the discipline of making frequent backup copies is too burdensome—until the day the disk is irrecoverably damaged (or physically lost), and weeks of work are lost. Using a centrally administered disk service facility solves most of this problem. There it is someone's assigned task to do backups, and the disks are usually sealed and well cared for, rather than resting in a desk drawer or knapsack.

The existence of a computer equipped with mass storage (disks) that provides a centralized file facility is also convenient for the users, as a user can access the desired data from any of the computers on the network. The user does not have to find a particular floppy in a particular desk drawer. A central disk service facility also reduces the problems associated with updating data stored in duplicate on several computer systems (distributed data bases). It is much more likely that everyone will be working from and updating the same data base.

A printer on each personal computer is often a needless expense, owing to their low utilization. Moreover, the quality of printers cheap enough to be provided with personal computers is often disappointingly low. Printer users have need for both distributed printers that are easy to walk to and central printers that are high in performance and quality.

A network of personal computers may also desire access to a public packet network or access to a company-owned satellite link. The high cost of such services and the low utilization by any one user suggest that they should be a shared resource that could be accessed over the network.

Finally, a word of caution is in order. Many books and magazine articles discuss local area networks strictly in terms of small personal computers sharing access to files, printers, and communication facilities. What's missing in this model is that large computers (mainframes) still have an important role in local area networks.

First, some problems cannot be solved on small machines. In particular, problems that require the rapid processing of a great amount of data, or processing very precisely expressed quantities, are best done on large, high-speed computers. Connecting such computers to local area networks and developing the appropriate network software makes that vital computational capability available to everyone.

Second, over twenty years ago, Herbert Grosch (then of IBM) postulated "Grosch's Law," which states that computational power rises as the square of the price paid; that is, for twice the price, one can get four times the power. This law has held fairly well, subject to the constraint that different packaging styles (a computer in a single integrated circuit versus a rack-mounted computer) have different cost curves. While Grosch's Law may apply only to constant classes of packaging, it is possible that the "cost per instruction per second" lines of large mainframes and personal computers may cross. It may be feasible to build a very large computer whose cost per instruction per second is lower than that of a microprocessor, and to divide the access to that machine by conventional timesharing techniques. People responsible for selecting computational capability for factories, laboratories, and colleges should not look solely at local area network solutions. A conventional batch system, a conventional timesharing system, or a hybrid arrangement with mainframes and personal computers on a local area network may provide the best approach.

In summary, local area networks are interesting and useful because they allow the users of terminals, small computers, and large computers to share access to common resources such as storage, input/output, and communication devices. In addition, they allow for shared access to information and permit personal communication between users.

2 Topologies and access methods

In a local area network, the relatively short distance spanned, the high bandwidth provided, and the low-cost media used create an operating environment in which "bandwidth is cheap," a substantial contrast to the traditional common carrier environment. An important consequence of these differing environments is that there are radical differences between the network topology (and the routing of traffic within that topology) for a telephone network and that for a local area network.

Local area network topologies

Whereas a telephone network generally has a hierarchical form, with links placed between nodes according to traffic and cost, a local area network usually has a very regular form that is either a star (Figure 4), a ring (Figure 5), or a bus (Figure 6). Further, the nodes of a telephone network route traffic according to complex rules, but the nodes of a local area network do very little (if any) routing.

Each topology shown in these figures is best suited to particular media types, has an optimum routing strategy, and has identifiable reliability characteristics, as will be described in the following paragraphs.

The star

The star is a convenient topology because it permits exceptionally easy routing; the central node knows the path to the other nodes. Since there is a central control point, access to the network can be easily controlled and priority status can be given to selected nodes. Last, but by no means least, a star configuration provides a central point for performing network maintenance and testing.

With the centralization of control come the requirements that the central node be exceptionally reliable and have the computational capacity to route all of the network traffic. These drawbacks have caused very few local area networks to be configured as true stars, but many utilize the star wiring pattern, as will be explained later.

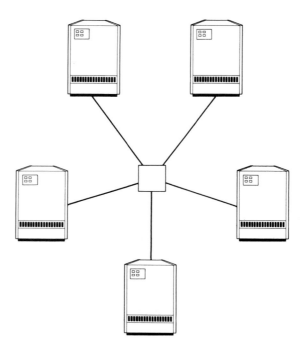

Figure 4. Star network

The ring

The ring is an attractive topology for transmission media that are simplex or difficult to tap, as all transmissions occur in one direction. The ring requires no routing, as each node (except the sender) always passes on a message. In addition, each node copies messages addressed to it. Ring systems have the unique feature that they can be arranged to provide reception verification. This is done by providing a bit in the message format that is complemented upon reception. Since a transmitted message in a ring eventually returns to the sender, the status of that bit can be checked to confirm reception, and the CRC (cyclic redundancy check) of the message can be examined to confirm that there were no transmission errors.

A ring may at first seem less robust than a star, as every node of a ring must work in order for the network to function correctly. In practice it is possible to design rings that allow a failed node to be bypassed via relays. This concept is shown in Figure 7. It is also possible to extend the bypass concept one step further and utilize bypass relays and duplex connections between the nodes. Such an arrangement allows a failed node or failed ring segment to be bypassed and is shown in Figure 8. The addition of a node to a ring network may pose a problem, however, in that the ring must be broken for the node to be inserted, causing the network to be out of service while such changes are made. The installation and testing of additional nodes can be sim-

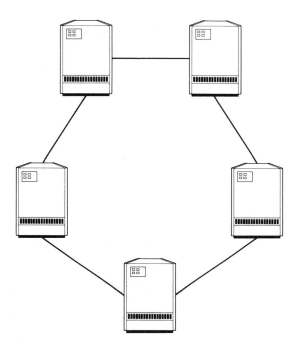

Figure 5. Ring network

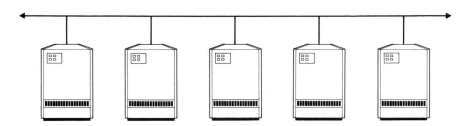

Figure 6. Bus network

plified by adding "wire centers" in which all of the bypass relays are located and to or from which all the node wiring is run (increasing the total length of the ring). A ring system with wire centers resembles a set of interconnected stars and is shown in Figure 9.

The bus

A bus requires a full duplex medium (one in which signals can flow in either direction). Unlike other topologies, nodes associated with a bus usually do no routing or message forwarding at all. That is because the bus is a broadcast medium in which all nodes receive all transmissions. Furthermore, in many bus systems the nodes contend with each

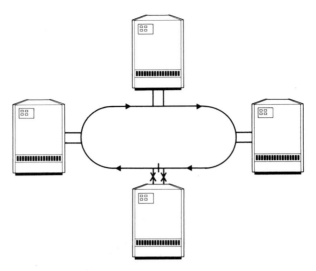

The connections for one node have been enlarged to show the bypass relay wiring. All nodes are similarly wired. Connections shown "X" are closed in normal operation.

Figure 7. Ring network with bypass relays

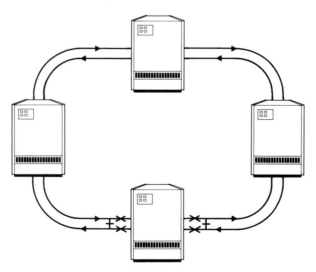

The connections for one node have been enlarged to show the bypass relay wiring. All nodes are similarly wired. Connections shown "X" are closed in normal operation. Connections shown "+" are closed in bypass operation.

Figure 8. Ring network with bypass relays between nodes

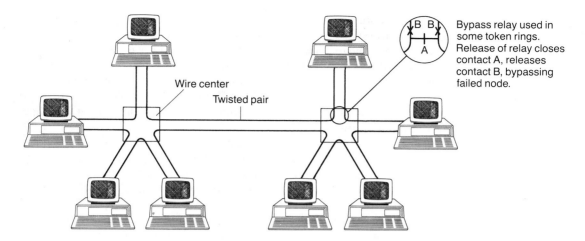

Wire center

Twisted pair

Bypass relay used in some token rings. Release of relay closes contact A, releases contact B, bypassing failed node.

Figure 9. Ring network with wire centers

other for use of the medium, a scheme which distributes the control of the medium to the nodes. The lack of routing and the lack of centralized control provide substantial reliability. A major attraction of a bus is that nodes can fail and traffic can still be passed over the network, provided the node failure is not of the "babbling tributary" type (in which random signals are applied to the line). Also, the addition of nodes can often be accomplished without disrupting network traffic.

Buses do have drawbacks, however. The impedance irregularities caused by the installation of taps will cause signal reflections that can interfere with data transmission if the taps are placed too close to each other. Thus, bus systems often have a minimum distance between taps specified in their installation manuals. In addition, physical damage to the bus sufficient to cause an impedance irregularity will also cause reflections. Finally, while bus systems often consist of segments separated by amplifying devices (repeaters—see Chapter 10), and the bus can be separated at these points for fault isolation purposes, segmenting the network for maintenance may be more difficult than with a star or wire-center-equipped ring network.

Circuit switching versus packet switching

Telephone networks and local area networks differ not only in physical ways, but also in how they are used. A telephone system is used by entering the number of the station to be called into an apparatus that can establish electrical connections between users—a switching system—which then sets up a connection. Every piece of information entered at the calling point is immediately conveyed to the called point with a delay determined only by the speed of light in the transmission medium used (wires, fiber optics, microwave radio). Further-

11

more, the connection between the calling and called points is used solely by the two communicating parties; although portions of the transmission system may be shared by several conversing parties, the parties will not notice that sharing (multiplexing) is occurring. The connection will continue to exist for exclusive use by the two communicating parties until they decide to "hang up." Providing the capability for any user to establish such a connection to any other user is called "circuit switching."

Circuit switching is an appropriate method for handling voice calls, as it provides the instantaneous, interactive, two-way communications so important to human interaction. However, when circuit switching is used for data transmission, some problems develop:

1. Data transmission has a very wide range of transmission rates—from hundreds of bits per second (between a terminal and a computer) to millions of bits per second (between computers). A switching system that provides circuit-switched connections should be able to handle the maximum transmission speed between all parties simultaneously, because that peak demand may occur and circuit-switched data cannot be delayed.
2. Data transmission is very bursty. Periods of peak transmission are followed by periods in which no data transfer takes place. Circuit-switched connections must remain in place during the periods of zero data transfer and be ready instantly to handle a transmission at the full data rate.

The differing characteristics between voice and data have prompted designers of data switching systems to move away from circuit switching toward special forms of message switching.

Message switching has been in use for many years, primarily for switching telegrams. An address is attached to the beginning of a message, which is sent to a switching center where it is stored. When facilities become available to send it on to another switching center closer to the destination, the message is forwarded over those facilities, to be stored at the next point. The storing and forwarding process continues until the message reaches its destination. Message switching is also called "store and forward" switching. Since a very long message could block other messages for an unacceptably long period of time, modern data transmission uses a variant of message switching, in which long messages are broken up into smaller pieces called packets. By limiting the length of the packets, the maximum delay that a message encounters in traversing the system can be reduced. This modern version of an old concept is called "packet switching."

For data transmission, packet switching is a lot more efficient than circuit switching because a circuit can be used for messages between several pairs of communicators simultaneously. If too many stations send data simultaneously, the data may be stored (buffered) and transmitted through the system after a slight delay.

Although efficient use of transmission channels is less important in local area networking than in long-distance data switching networks, efficient switching techniques can be important in local area networks, as the following example demonstrates.

Assume that a switching system to serve 1000 stations is to be designed. If each station can transmit and receive 100 Kbps, a circuit switching system must be able to switch 100,000 Kbps (100 Mbps). Alternatively, a packet switch could perform the above task over a 200 Kbps bus, assuming an arbitrary factor of two for packet formatting overhead (address, etc.), and a low duty cycle of data transmissions.

Since most local area networks are used primarily for data traffic, most local area networks use packet switching rather than circuit switching. The exceptions are PBXs, discussed in Chapter 3, and some broadband systems, discussed in Chapter 4. In the meantime, it is necessary to discuss the restrictions that packet switching places upon the methods used to control access to the transmission medium in local area networks.

Access control methods

Circuit switching systems acquire access to the transmission medium and send addressing information only at the beginning of a call, and several messages may be exchanged during a call. Packet switching systems, in contrast, require that the messages be broken up into packets and that the medium be accessed for each packet sent. The frequent need to access the medium in packet switching makes it important that the access control method used be quick and simple.

Another important difference between circuit and packet switching systems is that circuit switching systems provide the control necessary to set up connections by means of shared logic in the switching centers. Packet switching systems require that medium-access-control logic and addressing systems be located at each station. Thus, the complexity of the access control system plays an important role in system cost.

In summary, the advantages of packet switching systems must be weighed against their requirements, one of which is the need for quick, simple, low-cost logic in the stations for accessing the transmission medium.

While the previous sections have hinted at methods of controlling access to the media for various topologies, no control systems have been discussed in detail because there is not a one-to-one relation between control methods and local area network topology. Some methods are more widely used with certain topologies than others, so the following discussion of control methods will emphasize the most popular control/topology combinations.

Polling

All three topologies described above were used in teleprinter networks for military, weather, and airline reservation systems long before their appearance in local area networks. A widely used control scheme for such networks was "polling," in which a master station queried each slave station inquiring whether or not it had traffic to send. A polling system had the advantage that all stations could receive equal access, or priority stations could be given preference by having them polled more often. Polling systems were especially attractive in the applications listed because most of the complexity, expense, and maintenance needs were concentrated in a single point—the master station. Further, polling systems could function well over extremely long distances, since the reply-wait time could be adjusted to compensate for long propagation delays.

Polling was extremely time consuming, however, as a substantial number of the messages on the medium were polling messages from the master station. The success of a polling system was also highly dependent upon the reliability of the master station.

Tokens on a ring

An efficient variation of polling, especially suitable for the ring topology, is the use of tokens. In a token system, a special bit pattern referred to as the "token" circulates around the ring. If a node has no traffic, it allows the token to pass. If the node does have traffic, it takes the token, inserts a message in front of the token, and then reinserts the token. The token system provides the fairness and distance insensitivity of the polling system, but can utilize the medium more efficiently, since the token is passed along rather than always coming from a master station.

Token propagation relies upon the correct performance of the nodes, however, and provision must be made to recover gracefully (i.e., with minimum inconvenience to the network user) from failures that have caused the token to disappear.

There are a number of variations of the token scheme. Many of the variations are described in the references, but one of them, the use of tokens on a bus, deserves special attention.

Tokens on a bus

The function of a token passing from node to node on a bus is similar to its function on a ring; receipt of a token represents the "right to transmit." However, the token is passed from node to node in a different fashion. Rather than being passed from a node to the physically adjacent next node as it is on a ring, a token on a bus is passed from node to node by means of an addressing algorithm, such as passing the token to the node with the next lowest address.

If the node to which the token is addressed has no traffic, it forwards the token to the node with the next lowest address. If the node does have traffic, it takes the token, transmits a message, and then forwards the token.

So far, this sounds exactly like a token ring. However, in the area of reception monitoring and system integrity checking, there are some substantial differences. In a token bus system, the node which has just forwarded the token listens to make sure that the succeeding node has received the token and has begun transmitting. This listening process has to be carefully done, as in a system with long delay (for example, a broadband system where signals pass up to "headend" equipment at one end of the system and back), the next signal a node forwarding the token hears may be its own. It is important that the correct decision be made at this point, because assuming that the token has been correctly forwarded when it has not can result in a lost token. Incorrectly assuming that the token has been lost, and generating a new one, can result in two tokens being present.

Contention: ALOHA and slotted ALOHA

Another control technique is contention. While this technique is most suitable for a bus topology, the classic use of contention was the ALOHA network in Hawaii, a star topology. The ALOHA network used radio communications from widely scattered nodes to a central node. Although the central node could communicate with the outlying nodes, they could not communicate with each other. The control system chosen was that the outlying nodes would transmit whenever they wished. If no one else was transmitting during that time, the central node would receive the message correctly; otherwise, the reception would be garbled by a transmission from some other node, an occurrence referred to as "collision."

A possible analog of the ALOHA system is a meeting in which all of the participants talk to the chairman whenever they want. As might be imagined, the throughput of such a scheme is quite low—the medium is used for successful transmissions less than 20 percent of the time.

In the "talk whenever you want to" contention scheme, often referred to as "pure ALOHA," it is possible that a collision will occur at any time during a transmission. A collision can even occur at the very end of an otherwise good message, wasting the channel time it took to send that message. A substantial improvement in channel time utilization was accomplished by creating the "slotted ALOHA" contention scheme. In slotted ALOHA, the nodes are synchronized and only begin transmissions at the beginning of a time slot and can only transmit for at most the length of the slot time. As a result, some time slots contain a jumble of simultaneous transmissions, some contain no transmissions, and some contain the transmission from just one node—the successful transmissions.

Returning to the meeting analogy, it is as if the chairman only allowed people to talk for less than a minute, starting exactly on a minute boundary. Slotted ALOHA provides roughly twice the capacity of pure ALOHA; the medium is used for successful transmissions slightly less than 40 percent of the time.

Contention: CSMA and CSMA/CD

The contention systems decribed for the ALOHA network may seem strange, but the limitation that the nodes cannot hear each other is a severe constraint. If that constraint is removed, a number of more attractive techniques can be used, the simplest of which is "carrier sense multiple access," or CSMA. In CSMA, a node listens to the medium before transmitting; if nothing is heard, it begins transmitting. There is, however, a finite probability that some other node will come to the same decision at the same time, and two (or more) transmissions will start simultaneously. The likelihood of such an event increases on long buses, because a transmission can commence at one end of the bus and not propagate to the distant end of the bus before a node at the distant end decides to transmit. Thus an additional feature, collision detection, is usually added to CSMA systems to create "carrier sense multiple access with collision detection," or CSMA/CD. The collision detection may be accomplished by comparing transmitted data with received data to see if the message on the medium matches the one being transmitted or by using techniques which detect the presence of other transmissions by direct electrical means.

Returning to the analogy of a meeting, the comparison of transmitted and received data is the method actually used by meeting participants. A person listens to see if anyone else is talking. If not, he begins to talk while listening to see if the sounds in the room contain voices other than his. If another voice is heard, each speaker will usually "back off" by being silent for a few seconds, and then will try to start talking again.

In a CSMA/CD system, backing off when a collision is detected is also used. The amount of time before a retry can be random or can follow the "exponential back-off" rule. In random retry, a transmitting node which has encountered a collision will wait a random amount of time and then retry. If the retry encounters a collision, the process will be repeated using another random time interval. In exponential back-off, retries are made after random intervals, but each succeeding random number is chosen from random numbers that have twice the mean of those used for the previous attempt. This procedure is continued until either a collision-free transmission is accomplished or a maximum retry limit is exceeded. The optimum strategy for backing off has been the subject of a number of papers.

As with token bus and token ring systems, CSMA/CD has the advantage that control is distributed to the nodes, and in the bus topology, where the nodes are not part of the medium, a high degree of reliability is possible. However, use of CSMA/CD on its best-suited topology, a bus, is not without drawbacks. As mentioned above, two nodes that are beginning to transmit may not recognize each other's presence (i.e., detect collision) for some time, because of the amount of time (about 5 nanoseconds per meter) that it takes signals from each to reach the other. If the messages are short enough, a collision may occur without either node's knowing about it. Thus, CSMA/CD requires that messages not be less than a minimum length which is a function of the transmission speed and the length of the medium. Thus, this relationship places practical limits on the packet size and the medium length. Another problem in CSMA/CD is that the amount of time required to gain access to the medium is variable; in fact, there is theoretically no guarantee that a node will ever get a chance to transmit. This problem can generally be ignored in systems carrying less than about 40 percent of the medium capacity.

The preceding discussion of local area network topologies and control systems is intended only as an outline. The references listed below and the proceedings of recent conferences should be consulted for a complete and up-to-date view of progress in local area networks.

References

Binder, R.; Abramson, N.; Kuo, F.; Okinaka, A.; and Wax, D. "ALOHA Packet Broadcasting—A Retrospect." Proceedings, National Computer Conference, 1975, pp. 203–215.

Clark, David D.; Pogran, Kenneth T.; and Reed, David P. "An Introduction to Local Area Networks." Proceedings of the IEEE, November 1978, pp. 1497–1517.

Farber, David J. "A Ring Network." *Datamation*, February 1975, pp. 44–46.

Fraser, A. G. "Spider—An Experimental Data Communications System." Conference Record, International Conference on Communications, 1974, pp. 21F1–21F10.

Gordon, R. L.; Farr, W. W.; and Levine, P. "Ringnet: A Packet Switched Local Network with Decentralized Control." Proceedings, 4th Conference on Local Computer Networks, 1979, pp. 13–19.

IEEE Standards 802.1, 802.2, 802.3, 802.4.

Metcalfe, Robert M., and Boggs, David R. "Distributed Packet Switching for Local Computer Networks." Communications of the ACM, July 1976, pp. 395–404.

Rawson, Eric G., and Metcalfe, Robert M. "Fibernet: Multimode Optical Fibers for Local Computer Networks." IEEE Transactions on Communications, July 1978, pp. 983–990.

Thurber, Kenneth J., and Freeman, Harvey A. *Tutorial—Local Computer Networks*. IEEE Catalog No. EHO 163-6. New York: IEEE Computer Society, 1980. (Note: This publication contains reprints of most of the articles cited above, in addition to others not listed here.)

3   PBXs

Many people feel that local area networks are not limited to the topologies and access methods discussed in Chapter 2. An often discussed additional type of network is that provided by telephone switching equipment, specifically private branch exchanges (PBXs). This chapter explores the history, technical developments, and other characteristics of PBXs, and their use as local area networks.

PBX history

In movies depicting the typical office of the 1920s (the "Office of the Past"), an executive's desk was often littered with a half-dozen or more telephone instruments, each associated with a line to the local telephone exchange. With the advent of multiline telephone instruments with line selection buttons and call-hold circuitry, much of the desktop clutter disappeared. However, it was still the custom that all telephone lines serving a company appeared on all desks. This posed several problems, the most important being the treatment accorded the calling customer. Someone had to be assigned the task of answering any line that rang, greeting the caller, determining who was being called, and notifying that person that he should "pick up" the line on which the call had arrived.

The all-lines-at-all-desks scheme worked acceptably for small organizations in which everyone was in one room. As organizations became larger, however, it was necessary to add intercom systems that permitted the person answering the call to announce the call arrival to the intended recipient by calling that person over the intercom. The intercom system also permitted intercommunication among the office workers, a feature which became more important as the number of offices grew.

As organizations grew yet further, the traffic over the intercom system increased enormously, as did the inconvenience of talking to people within the company over one communications system and talking to people outside the company over another. In addition, the number of lines required to serve the company often grew beyond the number that could be accessed by the multibutton telephones on each desk.

The solution to these problems was a small telephone switching system ("exchange") that was connected to the main telephone company exchange (i.e., a "branch"), but whose telephone lines served only offices of one company (i.e., it was "private"). Such a system was referred to by the initials PBX, standing for *private branch exchange.*

In a private branch exchange, intercommunicating calls within the organization are switched via switching equipment located on the organization's premises. Persons desiring (and authorized) to make calls to locations outside the company facility do so by dialing a prefix code (usually 9) which causes the PBX to select an available line to the telephone company exchange. Incoming calls are usually answered by an operator whose initial duties in call handling are similar to those described earlier—greet the caller and determine to whom the caller wishes to speak. However, in the case of a PBX, the operator advances the call through the PBX to the desired party, rather than alerting the desired party via a separate intercom. The dial access to outside lines and the call switching capability of the operator eliminate the need for outside lines to appear at each desk, permitting the use of an arbitrary number of outside lines.

PBX technical developments

The technology used in PBXs has reflected that of their parents, the telephone company exchanges, although the technology used in small PBXs is sometimes more advanced than exchange technology. In the 1920s and early 1930s, many PBXs were manual, just as many exchanges were manual, but automation was gaining a strong foothold. This feature caused some to coin the acronym PABX, the *A* standing for "automatic."

By the 1940s, automatic switching was common in PBXs. Some used stepping switch designs, in which mechanical devices moved in step with the digits being dialed, while others used "all-relay" designs, in which the only mechanical motion was the operation of relays. By the 1950s, crossbar systems existed in both PBXs and main exchanges. These systems were the height of the electromechanical switching art, as the switches had minimal mechanical motion and were controlled by sophisticated relay logic (common control) shared among the switching elements.

In the 1960s it became evident that maintenance was an important problem with the preceding electromechanical designs, and that telephone users were willing to pay extra for special features such as abbreviated dialing, call forwarding, and three-way calling. Both the maintenance problem and the feature marketing opportunity could be addressed with a single solution that was then becoming available: electronics.

Although the first commercial electronic switching systems improved reliability and lowered maintenance costs by employing electronics, only the common control portion of these systems was electronic. The switching of the speech paths was accomplished by metallic contacts sealed in glass capsules. Since each call took a physically identifiable path, such a switching system became known as a "space division" switch.

Although experiments were conducted with switching techniques other than space division during the 1960s, it was not until the 1970s that other methods were successfully introduced into the marketplace. Time division multiplexing was the most important of these new methods, as it paved the way for the use of PBXs for data switching.

Time division multiplexing

More than fifty years ago, Harry Nyquist proved that an analog signal could be "sampled" (measured periodically) and then faithfully reconstructed from the samples if the sampling were done at a rate twice the highest frequency present in the analog signal.

Voice signals utilize frequencies less than 4000 Hertz. Thus, sampling a voice signal at 8000 Hertz is sufficient to create a string of pulses that can later be used to reconstruct the original voice signal. This process is shown in Figure 10.

However, the samples shown in Figure 10 are still analog—that is, they have an arbitrary number of amplitude values. A signal with so

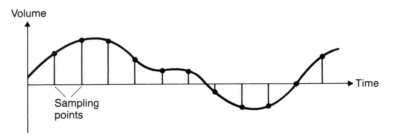

Figure 10. Sample of a voice signal

many possible values is difficult to reconstruct accurately when received over a noisy communication channel. It would be highly desirable to convert the signal into some type of digital representation—some combination of 1s and 0s—since a signal with only two values is easier to discern in the presence of noise (interfering electrical signals).

The encoding of analog pulses into digital values can be done by limiting the number of amplitude values to some number of discrete values. Each pulse is then assigned the binary code that represents the discrete amplitude value closest to the pulse's actual value. This process is diagramed in Figure 11, where the number of discrete amplitude levels has been limited to eight for clarity.

Close examination of Figure 11 reveals that errors are being introduced in the process of "quantifying" the analog signals into binary values; they are called "quantization errors." Quantization errors are reduced as the number of assignable discrete values is increased, because the difference between the signal's actual value and the nearest assignable value is reduced. However, an increase in the number of assignable discrete values means an increase in the number of binary bits needed to represent the signal being transmitted. Thus, the number of values chosen is a compromise between quantization error and transmission efficiency. In telephony, the number of values used is 256 and requires eight bits to represent a sample.

A voice signal that has been sampled at 8000 times per second, and encoded into 8-bit quantities produces a 64,000-bit-per-second data stream from which other electronic circuitry can restore an almost perfect replica of the original speech by a process called "decoding."

The encoding of speech into digital form, and the transmission of

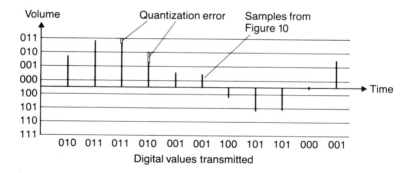

Figure 11. Digital coding of analog samples

multiple digitally encoded conversations over the same transmission facility, is the basis of time division multiplexing, which was first used in digital transmission systems introduced in the early 1960s. When the appropriate integrated circuits became available a decade later, time division multiplexing became attractive for both transmission and switching. The use of time division multiplexing for switching had the following advantages.

1. During the 1960s, a great many digital transmission systems had been installed between switching offices. A major expense associated with such systems had been the installation of "channel banks," which converted analog signals to digital and vice versa at the two ends of the transmission facility. With the advent of digital switching, signals could stay in digital form and channel banks were unnecessary until an analog switch or analog transmission facility was reached.

2. Time division switching could be accomplished by logically gating digital signals on to and off from a bus within the switching system. Additional traffic could be handled (to some degree) by increasing the bandwidth of the bus. It thus became possible to design a switch that permitted everyone to call everyone else. This type of switch design is referred to as "nonblocking." It contrasts with space-division switching designs, which generally do not permit more than about 20 percent of the users to be simultaneously engaged in calls.

3. The technology used for digital switching was the same integrated circuit technology which was enjoying such radical improvements in cost and performance in the computer industry.

While the first item on the list pertains primarily to the use of digital switching in telephone exchanges, the second and third items apply to both PBXs and telephone exchanges. In addition, there is another attribute of digital switching that is of special significance in PBXs:

Since digital switching systems carry voice as 64-Kbps bit streams, they can also carry a 64-Kbps data transmission for a cost identical to the cost of carrying a voice conversation.

This attribute is significant in thinking about local area networks, because it means that a digital PBX can put 64-Kbps data at everyone's desk very economically.

Use of a PBX as a local area network

Consider the two typical local area networks shown in Figure 12. In each part of the figure, a local area network (in one case a ring and in the other a bus) spans a distance D2 and consists of devices to which user terminals are attached via lines of length D1.

Those who think of local area networks as CSMA/CD buses will subconsciously assign the value of D1 as 5 meters, since terminals in CSMA/CD systems are usually close to terminal concentrators which connect the terminals to the CSMA/CD bus. They will also assign the value of D2 as being 500 meters, the distance typically spanned by a segment in Ethernet, a popular CSMA/CD system.

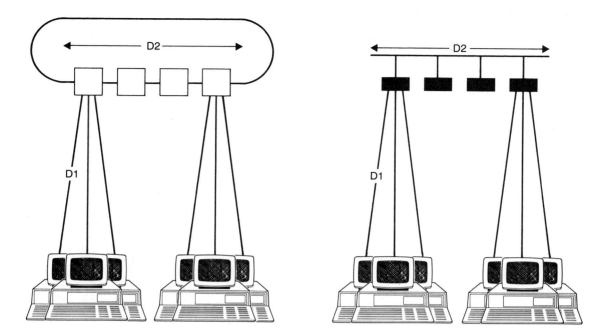

Figure 12. Two typical local area network configurations

People with a PBX background will assume that the distance D1 represents the lines from the PBX to the telephone/data stations and will assign a value of 500 meters. D2 is plainly the backplane bus of the PBX and is in the vicinity of 5 meters.

Looking at Figure 12, one may conclude that a PBX is the same thing as a ring or bus local area network, except for the relative lengths of the taps and the main digital pathway. However, there are some important differences between PBXs and other forms of local area network. These differences include wiring cost, blocking, bandwidth, reliability, services provided, standards, and circuit versus packet switching.

Wiring cost

One of the most attractive features of using a PBX as a local area network is the low cost of wiring. The low bandwidth used means that simple unshielded twisted pair can be used. Further, a long tradition of telephone wiring means that architects and contractors have already designed the building duct system to accommodate PBX wiring.

A few important points about the simplicity of PBX wiring need closer examination, however. First, it is not necessarily true that a new digital PBX can use the wiring that was previously installed for an older PBX. This is true only if the number of conductors available to the desks is sufficient, and only if the new PBX will work satisfactorily over a mixture of twisted pair and non-twisted "quad," the four-conductor wire that typically runs from a telephone instrument to the nearest junction box.

Second, it should be noted that other local area network systems can also use simple wiring. Ring systems frequently use shielded twisted pair, and bus systems can use shielded or unshielded twisted pairs between the user terminal and the terminal concentrator. In addition, wire centers for token rings or terminal concentrators for bus networks can be located in telephone equipment closets, thus taking advantage of the radial wiring plan of building ducts.

There is a basic tradeoff concerning wiring that applies for all types of local area network, including PBXs: If there is going to be very high bandwidth capability at the user terminal, the wiring to achieve that service will be costly or will have distance limitations. If only moderate speeds are required, more economical wiring plans can be used.

Blocking

The use of PBXs for data transmission in the early 1960s involved adding modems to the lines of existing analog space division switches. Data transmission over the modem-equipped lines was often more frequent and of longer duration than the voice calls for which the PBX had been designed. Blocking, the inability to place calls, was a frequent result.

The traffic handling capability of a PBX is often expressed in Erlangs per line during the busiest hour of the busiest day of the year. If a line is busy throughout the busy hour, that line is handling 1 Erlang of traffic. Another unit of traffic intensity used is hundred-call-seconds, for which the abbreviation is CCS. There are 3600 seconds in an hour, so 36 CCS equals 1 Erlang. If all of the lines in a PBX can handle 1 Erlang (or 36 CCS) of traffic during the busy hour, that PBX is non-blocking.

As explained above, modern time-division multiplex digital switches can be designed either to be nonblocking or to have a very low possibility of blocking. The choice between these alternatives is probably moot, as some percentage of the computer users in any organization are always on vacation, out sick, or for some other reason not using their terminals.

Bandwidth

The question of whether 64 Kbps is an adequate transmission speed is very complex. The arguments that 64 Kbps is inadequate include the following.

1. *Speed Inflation*

Twenty years ago, 110 bps was widely used, and anyone who had a 300-bps terminal enjoyed a great luxury. More recently, 9600 bps has been the norm, with some use of 19,200 bps. It seems safe to assume, based on a projection of this trend, that 64,000 bps will soon be the norm, and that speeds beyond that will be desired in a few years.

2. *Changing Applications*

The speeds mentioned above were for terminal to computer traffic. As personal computers replace terminals, traffic characteristics will be dominated by file transfers rather than the human–machine interaction characteristic of terminals. File transfers that take more than a few seconds will be deemed unacceptable. Personal computers and workstations will have to have their own disks, an expense which could have been avoided in many cases if a network capable of multimegabit transfer rates had been used.

3. *Graphics*

"A picture is worth a thousand words." The human mind is capable of absorbing a tremendous amount of information per second, and the best way to accomplish those high transfer rates is via graphical display. High-resolution, quickly updated graphical displays require data transfer rates of 1 Mbps and above.

Arguments that 64 Kbps is adequate include the following.

1. *Word Processing*

Most office work involves the preparation and distribution of memoranda. Some of this is currently done on typewriters, but more and more is being done on word processors, many of which have communication line connections to electronic mail systems. A 64-Kbps facility should be adequate, as a 24-line screen of 80 characters per line (1920 characters) could be sent in less than one-quarter second.

2. *Transfer of Small Files*

A 64-Kbps line will move 8000 bytes per second. Looking through the directories of the users who are going to be using the network, it may be found that their average file size is only ten 512-byte blocks; these could be moved in less than a second.

3. *Buffered Graphics*

Some graphics systems contain substantial buffers that allow for image rotation and other presentation-related tasks to take place within the graphics station. The communications line requirements of such systems may be well satisfied by a 64 Kbps line. (This argument becomes very complicated, as it involves tradeoffs between the costs of graphics controllers and graphics stations.)

In addition to the 64-Kbps capability discussed above, there are PBXs available which offer transmission speeds of 128 Kbps or more. If the transmission speeds are high enough (around 1 Mbps), file transfers and graphics services become possible through the PBX. However, such a PBX may be quite costly; blocking may be introduced because of the finite bandwidth of the backplane bus; and there may be unacceptable limitations on how far away a terminal can be placed from the PBX equipment.

Reliability

It is very difficult to compare the reliability of a PBX with the reliability of other forms of local area network. First, some PBXs consist of only a central switch, while others are constructed of distributed switch modules interconnected by another form of local area network technology. Second, some PBXs have been designed by people with a telephony background, while others have been designed by people with a computer background.

PBXs that consist of only a central switch have a central point of failure. Redundant parts, self-checking systems, watchdog timers, controllers which bid to handle calls and cease to bid when they fail, and other robust design techniques can minimize the danger of failure, but can never eliminate it. In addition, the physical environment can threaten the central switch in the form of fire or broken water pipes. A PBX with a distributed architecture is less prone to single point-of-failure problems, yet is plainly no more reliable than the local area network used to interconnect the switch modules. The probability of damage to that local area network, like damage to any other type of local area network, is increased by the fact that the network's most vital parts are spread about the network user's facility.

The backgrounds of the PBX designers also influence reliability. People with a telephony background have an almost religious fervor about reliability. They are haunted by the vision of someone with a heart attack or life-threatening wound attempting to use the telephone to summon aid; that telephone must work. In contrast, computer people come from an environment where the computer's dazzling performance when it is up more than compensates for a few hours a week spent for preventive maintenance or other down time. In view of their backgrounds, it seems likely that a telephone person will probably design a more reliable PBX than a computer person.

One thing upon which the manufacturers of both PBXs and other local area networks can probably agree is that the reliability of a single system handling both voice and data is much more critical than the reliability of separate voice and data systems.

Servers

If a PBX is to be truly a local area network, it must permit users to have shared access to such resources as file servers, print servers, and computation servers. File, print, and computation servers are described in other chapters, but two important notes about servers are appropriate in a discussion of PBXs. First, if the services provided in a local area network are going to involve large file transfers, the limited transmission rates of typical PBXs may be a problem. Second, if the services provided will involve many short transfers, PBX call setup time may be a problem.

Although there are some cautions about file, print, and computational services on a PBX, there are also some services for which a PBX is especially well suited. One of these is voice-annotated text, and the other is voice mail. Voice-annotated-text service permits a person reading a document to find a marker next to a particular paragraph and, upon pressing a button, to receive voice commentary about that paragraph. Voice mail allows callers to unanswered telephones to leave messages, and also permits the transmission of meeting reminders or other verbal prompts to specified people at specified times.

Standards

Unfortunately, the interfaces used by digital PBX manufacturers have not yet been standardized. The number of wires used between the PBX and user terminal can be two, three, or four pair. One of the pair may contain conventional analog signals and permit the connection of an ordinary telephone instrument, while the other pair(s) carries data, signaling, and power. An alternative is for the analog to digital conversions to take place in the telephone set and for all signals on the wires to be digital. Since this latter method increases the amount of logic in the telephone, the telephones used may be more costly than conventional telephones (although their higher percentage of electronic versus mechanical parts favors them in the long run). Electronic telephones must be also designed to be powered by the PBX in case of power failure, a feature already found in conventional analog sets.

In addition to simple telephone sets, all PBX manufacturers supply their own feature-filled telephone sets which make use of the intelligence of the PBX to light lamps or put text on display panels indicating lines in use, message waiting, calling number, and so on. The electrical characteristics and signaling (line protocols) used on the wiring from the PBX to such telephone sets is typically chosen by the manufacturer to make implementation of his particular "feature set" as simple as possible. Since these sets differ, the line protocols differ.

The connection of data equipment to PBXs also lacks standards (or has too many, depending upon how you look at it). Some PBX manufacturers provide an RS-232-C connection at the telephone set; others provide an RS-422 connection at the PBX equipment; others provide yet different arrangements.

Circuit switching versus packet switching

The original use of PBXs for data transmission was to connect terminals to timesharing systems. One of the appealing features about this arrangement was that the PBX did not care how many bits there were per character, what protocol was used, or any other details of data transmission. The PBX performed a simple circuit switching function.

Unfortunately, a circuit switching system for data transmission is a substantial design problem because data transmission has a very wide range of transmission rates and transmission duty cycle. Periods of peak transmission are followed by periods in which no data transfer takes place; yet circuit-switched connections must remain in place during the periods of zero data transfer but be ready instantly to handle a transmission at the full data rate.

Switching systems designed for data transmission usually avoid this problem by employing packet switching, a variant of store and forward message switching, in which long messages are broken up into packets. For data switching, packet switching is a lot more efficient than circuit switching because a circuit can be used for messages between several pairs of communicators simultaneously. Moreover, the switching system does not have to be designed to carry full rate transmissions between all stations simultaneously, but rather can rely upon the statistical properties of data communication.

In addition to more economical switch design, packet switching offers the opportunity for a terminal or workstation user to establish several logical connections simultaneously and display the results simultaneously in different areas of the screen referred to as "windows." Circuit switching would require some type of conference call arrangement to accomplish this, a system difficult for the terminal or workstation user to manipulate.

It is certainly possible for PBXs to offer packet switching capabilities in addition to their customary circuit switching capabilities. In fact, to allow access to many network services such as file services, print services, and gateways to public packet networks, the PBX should include a packet switching capability. However, adding these capabilities to PBXs can be quite costly, whereas other types of local area networks operate on a packet-switched basis as part of their basic design.

Summary

Although many questions arise in deciding whether to use a PBX to supply all or some of the services desired in a local area network, there are a great many questions associated with all forms of local area networking. Modern digital PBXs using time-division mutliplexing techniques are a good candidate for providing many of the functions associated with local area networks and should be carefully considered. In addition, a hybrid network involving both a PBX offering 64-Kb switched services and a bus or ring network offering 10-Mbps service might be the best answer.

References   Bellamy, John C. *Digital Telephony.* New York: John Wiley & Sons, 1982.

Flint, David C. *The Data Ring Main.* New York: John Wiley & Sons, 1983.

McNamara, John E. *Technical Aspects of Data Communication*, 2nd ed. Bedford, Mass.: Digital Press, 1982.

4   Media

Preceding chapters have discussed topologies and access methods for major types of local area network, but none of these discussions has tied the network topology, network access method, network operational methods, or any other aspect of the network to the transmission medium used. A possible exception was the identification of PBXs with twisted pair. The exclusion of media from the discussion has been intentional because rings, buses, and PBXs utilizing ALOHA, slotted ALOHA, tokens, CSMA, CSMA/CD, and circuit switching are available in almost all combinations on a wide variety of media.

In this chapter, the physical properties of various media will be discussed, and despite the variety of local area networks using each medium, the most common use will be identified. Each medium has its unique advantages and disadvantages, and these are additive to the other features of the local area network chosen.

Media suitable for local area networks divide into three categories: twisted pair wiring, coaxial cable, and optical fibers.

Twisted pair   Twisted pair, shown in Figure 13, consists of two copper conductors, each covered with insulation, usually polyvinyl chloride (PVC). The conductors used are typically 22 or 24 gauge. The two wires are twisted about each other so that each is equally exposed to interfering signals picked up from the environment. This feature is particularly important when differential transmission is used, because in differential transmission, information is conveyed by the difference in voltage between the two wires. If the signal voltage applied to one wire is V_1 volts and the signal voltage applied to the other is V_2, the signal being transmitted is $V_1 - V_2$. If an externally induced noise voltage V_n is coupled to the wires, the twisting causes V_n to be equally coupled onto both wires. Thus, the voltage on one wire will be $V_1 + V_n$, and the voltage on the other wire will be $V_2 + V_n$. The receiver will take the difference between the voltages, which is $V_1 + V_n - (V_2 + V_n) = V_1 - V_2$. The noise voltage has been subtracted out!

It is possible to construct cables which contain multiple twisted pairs within the same overall sheath. By varying the rate of twist of pairs relative to each other, called the "lay," it is possible to greatly reduce interference between transmissions on the various pairs ("crosstalk").

Twisted pair is available simply enclosed in an overall PVC sheath, with overall shielding, or with each pair individually shielded. Shielding increases the immunity to outside interference and may also be required if the circuitry driving the wire pair generates sufficient radio frequency interference (RFI) that shielding is necessary to comply with FCC regulations. Shielding has the disadvantage that it increases the cable capacitance per foot and hence reduces the top speed at which the signals can be applied to the cable.

Figure 13. Twisted pair

Twisted pair should not be confused with the four-wire cable commonly used in telephone wiring that is referred to as "quad." Quad consists of four wires, individually insulated and housed in a jacket which has been extruded onto the wires. The four wires in quad (red, green, yellow, and black) are *not* twisted, so their performance in noisy environments is not as good as twisted pair (usually color-coded blue with white, orange with white, etc.).

Twisted pair is used to connect telephone instruments, data terminals, and computers to PBX switching equipment. When the PBX switching equipment is centrally located, the wiring plan resembles a tree, with large cables of several hundred twisted pair branching to smaller cables that feed local distribution boxes from which two, three, or four twisted pair feed each desk. When the PBX uses distributed switching equipment, a ring- or bus-type local area network connects switching nodes that are located throughout the building to be served. From the switching nodes small cables of twisted pair feed the local distribution boxes.

Twisted pair, especially shielded twisted pair, is also used in ring networks to connect data equipment to wire centers. It can also be used in bus networks; in this case, it is used to connect data equipment to terminal concentrators.

The signaling rates used on twisted pair range up to 10 Mbps, but the crosstalk between pairs at such speeds requires that shielding be used between the opposite directions of transmission.

Twisted pair is easy to cut, strip, and terminate. It fits easily into modular office furniture and cable raceways, since it is the medium of choice for telephone service, and furniture designers and building architects understand how to provide for telephone wiring.

Local area networks utilizing twisted pair use the full frequency spectrum available on the pair as a single communications channel without modulating the signals used up to higher frequencies to establish more than one communications facility over the same transmission medium. Hence, they are examples of "baseband" rather than "broadband" local area networks.

Local area networks utilizing coaxial cables operate as baseband or broadband systems, as will be discussed below.

Coaxial cable

Coaxial cable, shown in Figure 14, consists of a copper conductor surrounded by insulation, which is in turn surrounded by a tube-shaped conductor of solid copper, solid aluminum, or metal braid. The outermost tube and the center conductor share the same axis of curvature, hence the term "coaxial."

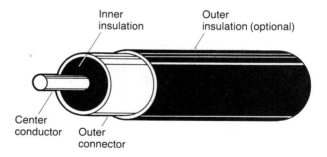

Figure 14. Coaxial cable

Use of coaxial cable in baseband systems

Baseband local area networks use the full frequency spectrum available on the cable without modulating the signals used to higher frequencies, hence the term "baseband." The ability to transfer low-frequency voltage levels, even DC voltages, is particularly important in a major application of coaxial cable in baseband systems, the Ethernet CSMA/CD system, where the DC voltage level is used to detect collisions.

The need for collision detection in CSMA/CD places another important restriction on the design of the cable: The cable's electrical char-

acteristics must ensure that signals travel through the cable rapidly—
that is, that they have a high propagation velocity. The role that propagation velocity plays in collision detection is explained below.

1. Effective use of collision detection requires that all stations know that a collision has occurred before they complete any message they are sending so that they will automatically retry the transmission of that message. If an automatic retry does not occur, firmware or software will have to detect the error and request retransmission, which is a much less efficient process.
2. In order that a station at one end of the medium detect a collision caused by a station at the other end of the medium, every message transmitted must be long enough to propagate the length of the medium, arriving at the far end just as the colliding station begins its transmission. In addition, the message must be still being sent as the collision condition propagates back to the sending station. In summary, the minimum message time must equal (or exceed) twice the propagation delay of the total length of the medium.
3. Ensuring that collision detection will work properly can be accomplished by making the minimum message size large (undesirable because of overhead), making the medium short (undesirable because of limited usefulness), or making the speed of propagation as close to the speed of light as possible.

Coaxial cable in CSMA/CD systems is specially constructed to have as high a propagation velocity as possible. This requires the use of foam core insulation between the center conductor and the outer conductor, a construction form that limits the minimum bending radius.

The relative cost of coaxial cable versus twisted pair for the construction of baseband systems is the subject of some controversy. Comparing prices in a wire catalog indicates that coaxial cable is much more expensive than twisted pair. The prices in the wire catalog may not matter, however, as installation costs and move-and-change costs for any local area network are high enough so that the catalog cost of the wire is generally unimportant. Coaxial cable is probably slightly more expensive to install than twisted pair, since it cannot be so easily installed in furniture or raceways, owing to its greater diameter and greater bending radius. However, coaxial cable systems using ring or bus topologies are probably less expensive than twisted-pair, point-to-point wiring for moves and changes, since all of the available bandwidth is everywhere, and someone who moves can often be simply reconnected to the ring or bus rather than rewired with new point-to-point wiring.

Both coaxial cable and shielded twisted pair provide excellent immunity to electrical interference and excellent compliance with FCC regulations for emitted radiation. Coaxial cable provides more bandwidth than shielded or unshielded twisted pair, however.

Use of coaxial cable in broadband systems

In addition to its use in baseband systems, coaxial cable can also be used in broadband systems, although a slightly different variety is required, and amplifiers are added.

When applied to local area networks, the word "broadband" usually refers to the use of community antenna television (CATV) technology to implement a local area network. CATV technology utilizes high-bandwidth coaxial cable that provides sufficient bandwidth (typically 300–400 megaHertz) for multiple local area networks, television transmission, and voice transmission, all in the same cable. Despite the great bandwidth, the cost of the cable and the associated fittings is remarkably modest because the same cable and fittings are used in thousands of CATV installations.

Since the role of the CATV industry has been so important in providing the technology and terminology used in broadband local area networks, a brief historical review is in order. CATV got its start in the early 1950s as a method of providing improved television reception to small communities where mountainous terrain or distance between the transmitting station and houses interfered with television reception. A collection of antennas suitable for the channels desired would be installed on a tower atop a tall hill or building. The signals received from the antennas would be combined, amplified, and otherwise conditioned in a nearby rack of electronics referred to as the headend. From the headend, cables would run down the streets of the town, hanging on the same poles as the power, telephone, and fire alarm wiring. The cables were run in a pattern best described as a "branching tree" (Figure 15), with the headend being the base of the tree, in the same fashion that the power substation, telephone exchange, and fire headquarters were the base of their respective distribution trees. At street intersections, a branch of the system would split off from the main trunk via a device called a "splitter." From the wiring on the poles, "drop wires" (a telephone term) were run to people's homes. The drop wires attached to the street wiring via "taps," which provided connection for four or eight drop wires. The wiring and taps attenuated the signal somewhat, so amplifiers were installed on various branches of the distribution tree.

In early CATV systems, the transmission system was unidirectional, as all of the transmission was from the antenna and associated headend equipment "downward" or "forward" to the subscribers' homes. More recent CATV systems have been installed with the capability of transmission from the subscribers' homes to the headend via an "upward" or "return" channel. The upward or return channel capability is achieved by installing bidirectional amplifiers on the various branches of the CATV distribution tree, and separating the directions of transmission on the cable by splitting the available bandwidth into two fre-

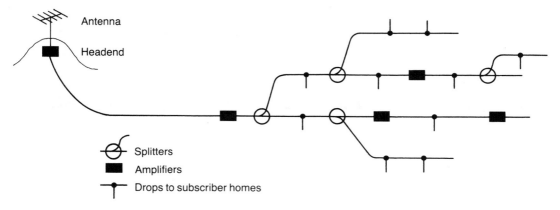

Figure 15. Community antenna television (CATV) system

quency bands, one for forward (headend to subscriber) transmission, and one for return (subcriber to headend) transmission.

Since the transmission from the subscriber to the headend is usually utility meter data or subscriber requests for specific video services, the return channel transmissions occur at substantially lower rate than the forward channel transmissions, which are full-bandwidth color television transmissions. Thus, CATV systems usually split the frequency assignments on the cable by assigning the frequencies between 5 and 32 megaHertz to the return channel and the frequencies between 54 and 300 megaHertz to the forward channel. This is called a "subsplit" frequency assignment and is shown in Figure 16. The frequencies between 32 and 54 megaHertz are unused because the filters used to select between the forward and return groups of frequencies are not perfect and require this band of frequencies as a "guard band."

When CATV technology is used to implement a local area network, however, one assumes that there will be an equal number of transmissions between all points in the network. To accommodate this, it is appropriate to assign the frequencies between 5 and 116 megaHertz to the return channel and the frequencies between 168 and 300 mega-Hertz to the forward channel. This is called a "midsplit" frequency assignment and is shown in Figure 17.

A third possibility is to provide separate cables for the two directions of transmission, a technique diagramed in Figure 18. The two-cable system has the benefit of having no headend equipment and no need for guard bands between the forward and return transmissions. Each direction of transmission has the entire bandwidth of a cable available. Separate amplifiers are required for forward and return transmissions in the single-cable systems, and the dual-cable system requires the same number of amplifiers, but eliminates the need for filters that separate the transmission directions.

The dual-cable system has some disadvantages, however. It requires

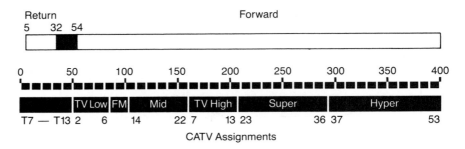

Figure 16. Subsplit frequency assignment

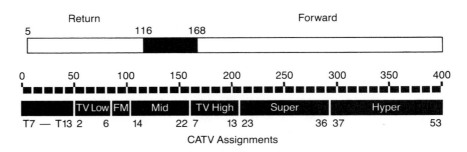

Figure 17. Midsplit frequency assignment

twice as much cable, twice as many splitters, and twice as many taps as a single-cable system.

As mentioned above, coaxial cabling is more expensive and difficult to install than twisted pair. However, the use of coaxial cable to achieve a broadband distribution system offers a tremendous amount of bandwidth. Since a major part of cable installation costs is labor, it could be argued that broadband is the best of all the choices mentioned so far, as it gives the highest bandwidth. Best of all, that bandwidth can be used for local area networking and a multiplicity of other purposes.

As with all apparent panaceas, one must pay for the flexibility of broadband. One of the ways in which one pays is with an increased planning burden. All local area networks require planning, but broadband especially requires planning and a great deal of up-front engineering. Signal levels throughout the system must be carefully calculated, and this requires that the length of cables, location of taps and splitters, and locations of amplifiers be precisely known. It is not necessary to plan or install the entire system all at once, but certain precautions should be taken.

Wherever it is likely that a branch of the distribution tree will be installed at a future time, for example to a new building, a splitter should be installed, with the unused port terminated. In this way, the

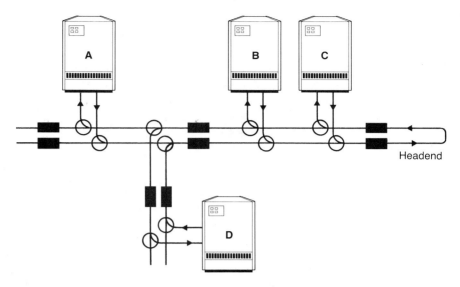

Figure 18. Dual-cable broadband system

transmission losses caused by the splitter will be included in the initial design, and the new branch can be added later without reengineering or readjusting the main system.

In a similar fashion, taps should be installed in such a fashion that there will be one drop per office. As a further precaution, each tap should have only about three-quarters of its drops used, leaving drop wiring capability for future expansion.

The reason for these precautions is that broadband cable fittings (splitters and taps) split the received power. This occurs because the impedance, an electrical property similar to resistance but varying with frequency, is equal for signals traveling farther along the cable and for signals branching off at the tap. Equal amounts of signal power take each path. This is in contrast to the high-impedance connection made by a baseband transceiver, where only a minuscule amount of the signal is delivered to the transceiver. The benefit of the broadband power-splitting arrangement is that the impedance of the distribution system branch added by a splitter, or user drop added by a tap, is identical to that which existed before the splitter or tap was added. The unchanging impedance allows splitters and taps to be added without fear of signal reflections and permits the added branches and drops to be of substantial length.

In contrast, taps in baseband systems connect to transceivers whose impedance is much higher than that of the main cable. Adding such taps causes impedance discontinuities, and thus taps must not be placed too close together or reflected signals may create transmission problems. In addition, the length of the cable stub from the tap to the transceiver must be limited.

The baseband system does have important advantages, however. Since the transceivers are high impedance, they can be added and removed from the system without affecting the signal levels. Broadband systems match the impedance, but they split the signal power in so doing. Thus, addition of a broadband splitter of tap halves the power of the received signal.

Because broadband cable additions can halve the signal power to the remaining portions of the system, the above precautions of engineering the system with additional capacity must be taken, or else the addition of splitters and taps will require reengineering the transmission levels in the system.

A final consideration with broadband is modem cost. It seems likely that broadband modems will always be more expensive than baseband transceivers. The reason is that with baseband, the transceiver does not need filters to select a particular channel for reception. Likewise, it does not need filters to limit its transmission to a particular channel.

Modem cost is especially noticeable in broadband systems which use "frequency agile" modems. Frequency agile modems, as the name implies, can change the frequencies they use for transmission and reception on the broadband system. The ability of the modems to select an idle channel provides a circuit switching capability. The issue of modem cost is not entirely tilted against broadband, however. In a broadband system, taps and their associated stubs are part of the design, and prewiring of offices means preinstallation of taps, into which the user subsequently plugs the modem whenever required. In baseband systems, tranceivers must be mounted close to or on the coax because of electrical considerations (reflections from "stubs"). Since transceiver installation is not a task for the untrained, either transceivers must be preinstalled, which is very costly, or there must be continual placement of transceivers as office requirements change.

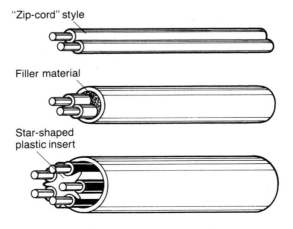

Figure 19. Fiber optic cables

Optical fibers Optical fibers, shown in Figure 19, combine the compactness of twisted pair with bandwidth which exceeds that of broadband coaxial cable. Their most appealing feature is that they experience very little electrical interference, even from lightning strikes. In addition, they operate well even when the ground potential between various buildings varies widely.

The inability of optical fibers to transmit DC voltages, an attractive feature when it comes to ground potential differences, makes their use in CSMA/CD systems difficult, and complicates their use in ring systems that utilize DC voltages to control the operation of bypass relays. Optical fibers are used between bus segments in Ethernet systems and between wire centers in ring systems. Furthermore, any local area network can be equipped with an interface to which terminals, workstations, and computers can connect via point-to-point fiber optic links (see Figure 20).

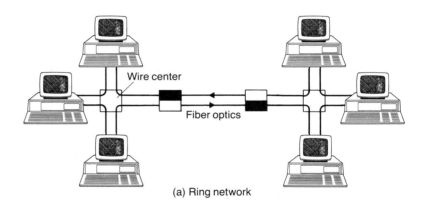

(a) Ring network

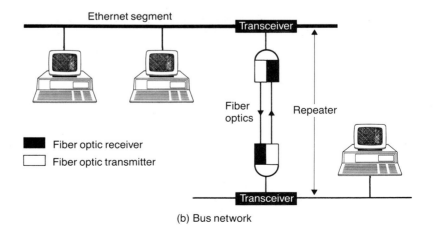

(b) Bus network

Figure 20. Local area networks with fiber optic links

The very low signal levels used in optical fiber systems required the use of receiver logic which was initially expensive and whose electrical connections had to be carefully engineered. However, substantial progress in making optical fiber systems cheap and easy to construct is being made, and the high bandwidth, small size, good bending radius, and robustness of these systems in noisy environments may yet revolutionize the local area network industry.

Summary

Local area networks can be constructed from media ranging from twisted pair to optical fibers. Throughout this range, the broader bandwidth media average the medium installation cost over a greater range of possible uses, but do so with associated increases in interfacing costs. It seems likely that the most cost-effective local area networks will probably use a variety of media, each cost optimized to its particular application.

5   Physical considerations

At one time, installing a data communication system meant either running twisted pair from terminals to a nearby computer or connecting equipment to distant points via modems. In both cases, a small amount of wiring was involved. In the former case, a few hundred feet of wire was run on the floor or stapled to the wall. In the latter case, a few feet of cable connected to the modem, after which the details of data transmission were the telephone company's problem.

With the advent of local area networks, computer and terminal manufacturers and their customers are finding themselves in the data transmission business, probably to a greater extent than they desire.

This chapter is intended as a guide to some issues that must be considered in planning and installing a local area network. It is not the intent of this chapter to be a complete installation guide for the major types of local area network. Rather, it is hoped that a discussion of physical factors will assist in local area network selection and protect the reader from unforeseen surprises once installation is under way.

Topology

Since the topology of a local area network has an influence on the problems which may be encountered during installation, some of the physical properties of various topologies need to be reviewed here.

Star-wired networks

Star-wired networks include local area networks with a central controller, ring networks that utilize wire centers, and PBXs that have a single switching point. Star-wired networks have the benefit that they are easy to service, since service personnel usually need only visit the failing station and the central point. They are also easy to expand, since installation personnel need only add a single link from the central point to the new service location, a task which does not generally disrupt the existing service. The drawbacks to star-wired networks are that a substantial amount of wire is required to link each station to the central point and the wiring space near the central point may become congested.

Ring-wired networks

Ring networks can be wired in the form of a true ring; that is, each station is wired directly from the preceding station and is wired directly to the succeeding station on the ring via the shortest physical path. This has the benefit of greatly reducing the amount of cable required compared with a star-wired ring, and will decrease the propagation time of signals around the ring. The disadvantage of this wiring style is that it is difficult to service, and new stations cannot be added without substantially altering the existing wiring pattern and hence substantially disrupting network operations.

Bus networks

Bus networks consist of a single cable to which stations attach as taps. Of all the network topologies, bus networks use the least amount of cable because they have a simple linear layout. However, servicing may be difficult since a fault could be introduced at any point, and adding stations may require adding length, which may require the addition of signal regeneration devices or other apparatus into existing portions of the network.

Cable distribution systems

Regardless of the local area network topology chosen, the cabling used to install the network must be placed in some housing or routing mechanism that will guide and protect the cable. The principal types of cabling systems are the following:

> Cable trays
> Hung ceiling
> Conduit
> Under-floor duct
> Cellular floor
> Raised floor

Cable trays

Cable trays (Figure 21) are often used in laboratories and other locations where frequent cable rearrangement is necessary and aesthetics is not a factor.

Hung ceiling

In a hung ceiling system (Figure 22), cables are routed in the space between the visable ceiling and the actual ceiling. The cables are brought down to the user locations either at the walls or via poles built especially for the purpose. Cables routed in this fashion can follow the shortest route to their destination and can be installed and removed with relative ease. The installation and removal of cables may damage other cables, however, and the dirt and disruption created by maintenance personnel working on ladders during office hours may reduce the efficiency of workers. While the hung ceiling distribution

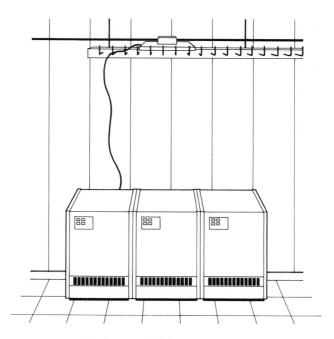

Figure 21. Cable-tray system

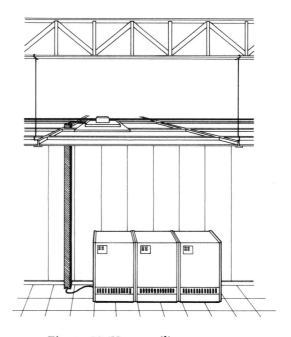

Figure 22. Hung-ceiling system

system is among the cheapest, the cable used may be expensive if the area above the ceiling is part of the building ventilation system. Fire codes may require that flame-retardant (Teflon) cables be used.

Conduit

Conduit systems may be either embedded in concrete or attached to building walls. Conduit systems offer the maximum in physical protection for communications cables, but are expensive to install and require careful planning. Among the planning tasks are making sure that the conduit cross-section is adequate (at least twice the cable cross-section) and making sure that no run contains more than two 90-degree bends unless pull boxes are installed. A further disadvantage of conduit systems is the difficulty in making modifications. Systems in which the conduits are exposed on walls can be modified with fair ease, but systems in which the conduit is in concrete are nearly impossible to alter.

Under-floor duct

Under-floor ducts (Figure 23) are long metal boxes running in the floors. A typical duct system utilizes large ducts running down hallways with smaller ducts intersecting every several feet. The smaller ducts run under the office floors and are accessable via service fittings which project from the floor under desks. Like conduit systems, under-floor ducts protect the cables from physical harm. Unlike conduit systems, fittings for routing wires into and out of the ducts can be installed and removed fairly easily. Under-floor-duct systems are expensive to install and difficult to expand. Moreover, the duct locations and associated service fittings limit furniture arrangement flexibility.

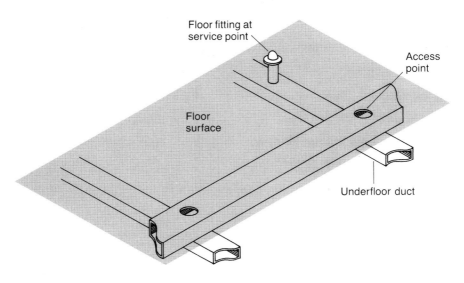

Figure 23. Under-floor-duct system

Cellular floor

A cellular floor (Figure 24) consists of distribution cells that are long, narrow troughs of metal or concrete running the length or width of the building. The spacing of these cells can be as close as one foot center to center, hence the coverage is much denser than under-floor duct. Running perpendicular to and above these cells are "trench headers," which are flush with the finished floor. The trench headers have openings in the bottom to connect with the distribution cells and removable covers on top to allow access from floor level. Cellular floors are similar in cost to under-floor duct systems but offer greater flexibility. Their sole drawback relative to under-floor ducts is that the service fittings are more difficult to install.

Raised floor

Raised floors (Figure 25) consist of removable metal panels set on a metal gridwork above the actual building floor. Commonly used in rooms designed for large computers, raised flooring offers the ultimate in flexibility, but also the ultimate in cost. The high costs are not only for the flooring itself, but also for constructing ramps at doors that lead to hallways or other rooms not so equipped, and for placing all electrical service in conduit.

Selection of a cable distribution system

If the building where the local area network is to be installed has not yet been constructed, consultation with the other people requiring service, such as the telephone and electrical groups in the organization, may yield a distribution system that is optimal for all. If the local area network is being installed in an existing building, the choices are far more limited.

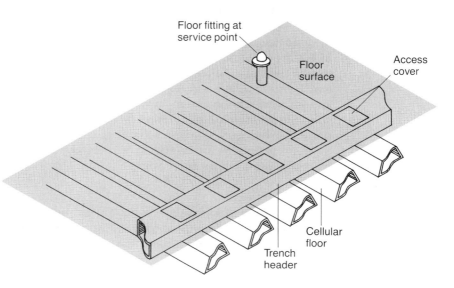

Figure 24. Cellular-floor system

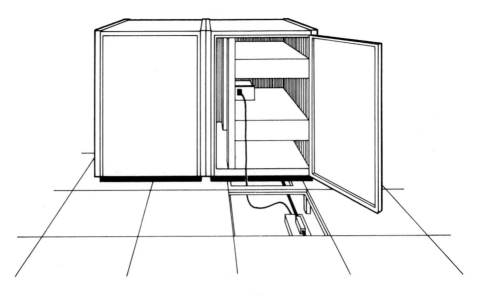

Figure 25. Raised-floor system

The issues of expandability and ease of moving service points cannot be overemphasized. All distribution systems have a maximum capacity, and that maximum capacity is often lower than one might at first estimate. The distribution system chosen should be installable with adequate capacity for all reasonably anticipated future growth.

Changes in service arrangements are also an important aspect. It is fairly common in some businesses for 50 percent of the telephones and data terminals to be moved every year.

The selection of a cable distribution system may also affect the type of cable selected. For example, some cable runs may be directly buried in the ground and require "direct burial" cable that is chemical- and rodent-resistant. Other cable runs may require "aerial and duct" cable which has strength and chemical characteristics appropriate to those applications. The locations in which the cable are run may require special fire-retardant properties, or other properties specified by the particular industry for which the installation is being done.

The remainder of this chapter is divided into four parts: site survey, planning, installation, and testing.

Site survey
The role of the site survey is to document the requirements and limitations that will influence the planning process. The site survey identifies the locations of equipment that is to be connected to the network ("service points" or "stations"), both in the near and long term, and identifies characteristics of the building construction, such as floor-to-floor riser locations, that pose constraints on the network layout.

In many ways, the site survey is an evaluation for installation feasibility. A very large site cannot be spanned by some forms of local area network. A site with many stations cannot be served by a network that has limited addressing capability. The discovery that some parameter of the intended network has been exceeded may force the choice of another network, may require modification of the network plan, or may require the selection of a hybrid network (see Chapter 10).

The first steps in the site survey are political, legal, and administrative, rather than technical. The process begins by contacting those people who have an interest in the project and whose assistance will be required for its successful completion. These include the facility manager for the buildings involved, HVAC (heating, ventilation, and air conditioning) personnel, and locally licensed electricians. One of the first questions to be asked of the facility manager is whether the building is owned or leased by the organization for which the network is being installed. The answer to this question may pose restrictions on the type of cabling (if any) that can be installed, the people who install the network, and the type of approvals needed.

The next questions to be considered concern building construction. The type of cable distribution system may affect the feasibility of installing some types of network. For example, while raised flooring is sufficiently flexible to accommodate any type of network, some underfloor duct and cellular systems have insufficient space for the bending radii required by baseband and broadband cables.

After considering these major items, the next step is to mark building plans with the locations of near-term and long-term service requirement points. Artifacts of the cable distribution system such as duct locations, riser locations, wiring closet locations, riser poles from offices to hung ceilings, and so on, should be recorded. In addition, special situations such as fire walls, unusual temperature areas, high humidity areas, and areas requiring fire-retardant cabling (check local codes), should be marked.

A physical survey of the site should be undertaken to ensure that there is sufficient room in the cable distribution system to accommodate the local area network wiring. Small details such as whether preterminated cables can be fished through the floor-to-floor risers and floor-to-ceiling riser poles must be checked.

During the physical survey, some of the questions to be asked depend on the type of local area network being contemplated. For example, in star-wired networks using wiring closets, the availability of power outlets, floor space, and wall space need to be checked. In bus systems requiring transceivers, space and convenient access to prospective transceiver locations should be checked. (The actual locations will be chosen during the planning process, but limitations on prospective locations should be noted during the site survey.)

Some local area networks have grounding requirements. The provision of ground bars in wiring closets or the availability of a suitable ground for coaxial systems must be checked. In multibuilding installations, the potential difference between grounds in various buildings must be determined and compared with network specifications. One should also remember that ground potential differences are not static. They may change substantially if one building is hit by lightning or a power surge occurs. If this is likely, isolating the local area networks in the two buildings by means of a fiber optic link should be considered.

Planning

Planning combines the data gathered in the site survey with the configuration rules of the local area network to determine cable runs, transceiver or modem placement, and so forth. The planning effort results in a Network Plan, which lists the required parts and details the appropriate procedures for installing the network. A good Network Plan can be used by a contractor who has never installed a local area network and still have satisfactory results.

In the following paragraphs, planning for two specific types of local area network are explored in detail. The examples chosen are radially wired networks, which typically use twisted pair, and bus-wired networks, which typically use coaxial cable.

Planning radially wired installations

A PBX that utilizes a single switching point, rather than distributed switching, is an example of a radially wired system. In a PBX installation of that type, an area of floor space must be set aside for the switching equipment and the associated wiring termination panels. The PBX vendor will usually specify that the area have temperature and humidity characteristics similar to those of an office environment, although some PBXs can stand more extreme conditions. For reasons of security, convenient maintenance access, and general reliability, the PBX area should not be used for other purposes (such as janitorial storage) and should be locked.

To minimize total wire runs, the PBX should be centrally located, although "central" in a spatial sense and "central" in terms of the building's cable distribution system may not be the same. In terms of the cable distribution system, "central" may mean "in the basement." A PBX system that has applications processors coupled to it may have to be located in a computer room, and any restrictions on placement of the PBX and placement of the processors should be checked during the planning phase. If a basement location is chosen, special care should be taken to ensure that flooding from broken pipes and similar hazards do not endanger the PBX.

Once the switching equipment location has been chosen, the next task is to plan the wiring pattern. Typical PBX wiring is in the pattern of a branching tree, as shown in Figure 26.

Various sizes of cable are available to provide the wiring pattern shown in the figure, and termination facilities are available in a wide

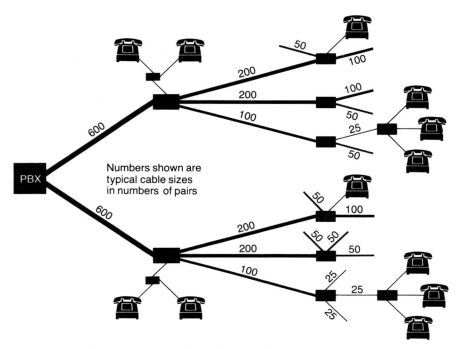

Figure 26. PBX wiring in branching-tree pattern

variety of sizes. As with the switching equipment, maintenance, security, and reliability considerations suggest that terminations serving larger areas should be protected by being placed in locked closets. This is especially the case when the wiring closets not only serve as distribution points but also contain network-related equipment ("wire centers"), as will be discussed below.

In addition to PBXs, star-wired rings (notably some token rings) also use radial wiring. In this type of network, stations are interconnected via wire centers, which are in turn interconnected. The general pattern is shown in Figure 27.

Since twisted pair are used, the planning for these networks is similar to that for PBXs, except that some interesting special cases can be accommodated. In particular, interbuilding wiring can be replaced by fiber optic links that interconnect the wire centers in a way which is free from electrical interference.

There are some additional considerations in preparing a Network Plan for a radially wired system:

1. The Network Plan should include explicit instructions and materials for penetrating fire walls and restoring their fireproof properties in approved fashion. Generally this means metal sleeves through the wall and special plugs that fill the space between the cable and the sleeve.

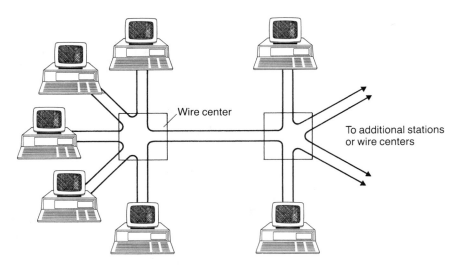

Figure 27. Ring network with wire centers

2. The Network Plan should include explicit instructions and materials for identifying the cables, recording the wire center locations, recording the points served, recording access points, etc.

3. It is usually possible to order cables in lengths long enough so that no splices are required. If splices are required, there should be as few as possible, and they must not occur inside conduits or in other inaccessable locations.

4. The Network Plan should include the preparation of wiring closets for terminal block installation. Typically, walls supporting terminal blocks must be covered with plywood or similar material. The network planner must determine whether this is required and determine who is to do this work, as it is often done by carpenters associated with the building rather than by the network installers.

Planning bus-wired coaxial cable systems

The first step in laying out cable runs for a coaxial cable system is to take the floor plans created by the site survey and mark a circle around each point at which a connection to the network is required. The diameter of the circle depends upon the type of system being installed. For example, in Ethernet there is a limit of 50 meters on the length of cable connecting a device to its associated transceiver. Allowing for cable length within the device enclosure, vertical distances, movement to various corners of the office, and a safety margin, a limit of 20 meters might be chosen for the radius of the circle. After the circles have been drawn, an attempt is made to place the main cable so that it touches or intersects all of the circles.

If the building is narrow, the system planner can maximize the floor area covered by the proposed coaxial cable path by running the cable down a central hallway. Such a cable run also provides convenient access to the transceivers. Figure 28 shows a sketch of such a system.

In buildings which have a number of wings, each wing could have a system laid out as shown in Figure 28. This would produce a layout as shown in Figure 29. The bus in each wing of the building is connected to the bus running down the main corridor by means of a signal re-generation device called a "repeater." The layout shown in Figure 29 could also be used to cover a single large floor of a building or several floors in a multistory building.

Three possible problems can arise in configuring a bus system. One is the case where a few stations are located far from the main coaxial cable run. There are several solutions to this problem. First, it may still be possible to reach the distant stations if careful measurements are

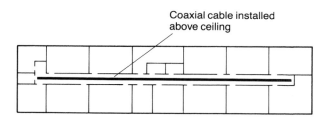

Figure 28. Coaxial-cable run in a central hallway

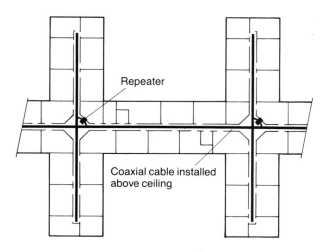

Figure 29. Wiring scheme for a building with several wings

made; that is, make the diameters of the circles drawn about the service points exactly according to specifications—with no safety margin. Alternatively, the main cable run can be diverted to reach the distant stations.

A second problem arises when the configuration of stations strains the physical limits of the network. To attack this problem, the network should be arranged so that the main coaxial cable travels in as straight a line as possible, despite having to leave the convenience of corridors. In addition, the distances allowed between the cable and the service points should be less conservative than distances suggested previously. This ability to trade off between main coaxial cable length and drop cable length is an important and helpful aspect of bus network design. In the process of straightening the coaxial cable run, it may be discovered that relocation of a particular riser, or removal of some physical obstacle, would allow the network to span the service points. In that case, the site survey personnel and facilities manager should be contacted and the feasibility of making those building changes studied. Finally, it might be necessary to establish separate networks interconnected by repeaters, bridges, or gateways, devices that are discussed in greater detail in Chapter 10.

A third problem area occurs in networks that have restrictions on the minimum spacing between taps. If a large number of stations are to be served in a small area, it will be necessary to allow extra cable length so that extra taps can be installed. An example of this is shown in Figure 30. An alternative arrangment used in some systems is a device which allows eight stations to use a single tap. This is shown in Figure 31.

Once a path for the coaxial cable has been established, the path of the cable, the coaxial cable section lengths, and the taps locations are

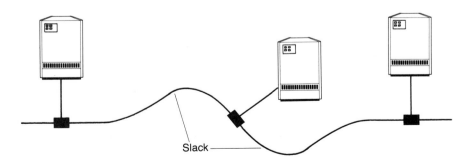

Slack

Figure 30. Plan providing adequate tab spacing

marked on the floor plan. Provisions for securing the cable and taps via cable ties should also be noted.

Some additional considerations in preparing a Network Plan for a bus system are as follows:

1. Bus systems require terminators at each end. These terminators should be conveniently available for maintenance personnel to attach test gear, i.e., at or near floor level. They should be protected from tampering, however.
2. High-rise buildings with a doughnut-shaped work area surrounding a service core should have a doughnut-shaped coaxial cable layout on each floor, with the ends of the bus run occurring at the floor-to-floor riser location.
3. As with radially wired networks, the Network Plan for a bus network should include explicit instructions and materials for penetrating fire walls and restoring their fireproof properties in approved fashion.
4. While coaxial cables may be able to stand temperature extremes from $-18°C$ to $150°C$, some devices (such as transceivers) will typically have much narrower limits (such as $5°$ to $50°C$) because of their electronics content. The system planner should be aware of these limitations when reviewing the "excessive conditions" areas noted on the site survey.
5. As with radially wired networks, the Network Plan for a bus network should include explicit instructions and materials for identifying the

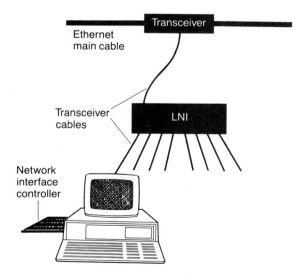

Figure 31. Eight stations sharing a tap

cables, recording the transceiver locations, recording the points served, recording access points, etc.

6. The network planner must be aware, and must ensure that the network installer is aware, of bend radius restrictions. For Ethernet installations, these are 5 cm for conventional transceiver cables, 10 cm for flame-retardant transceiver cables, and 20 cm for the main coaxial cable. Similar restrictions apply to broadband coaxial cable.

Installation

During installation the Network Plan guides the actual process of installing the local area network. The Network Plan, via a bill of materials, has provided cables, cable connector hardware, transceivers or modems, system-grounding components, and installation tools. The Network Plan has also provided marked floor plans, schematics, and site-specific notes.

The first step in installation is to make any additions or modifications necessary to the building's cable distribution system, such as the addition of interfloor sleeves.

In systems using terminal blocks, the blocks should be mounted in the wiring closets before the cables are installed so that this work will not have to be done amid a forest of unterminated cables.

Once the cable distribution system is ready to receive the cable, cable installation begins. It would be wise for the network planner to supervise this task in some way to ensure that proper precautions in cable handling are taken.

In coaxial cabling systems, grounding is important. Thus, the conductive components, such as barrel connectors, should include insulating sleeves to ensure that the system is grounded only at the point intended as network ground. The network ground connection is accomplished with a clamp on a designated barrel connector or terminator. Further details may be found in the references.

Testing the installed network

Testing will be required after installation, whenever the network is expanded or reconfigured, and when maintenance is indicated. The tests include verification of the physical channel, testing the modems or transceivers, and testing the ground system.

Test equipment

The type of test equipment required varies with the type of network installed. Since DC continuity, or the lack thereof, is an important factor in the analysis of many networks, a volt-ohm-meter (VOM) is a useful tool. In a PBX system, a lineman's test set (basically a telephone handset with built-in dial) is a very useful testing aid. In a coaxial cable system, a time domain reflectometer is often useful. In addition, testing of the grounding system may require an electrician's clamp-on ammeter capable of reading a 10 milliampere current accurately.

***Testing
a radially wired
system***

The customary first test of a PBX is for a roving test person to go to each location at which a telephone has been installed and see if dial tone can be obtained. After obtaining dial tone, the test person dials a designated test number, which is answered by a "central test" person. After establishing that satisfactory transmission can take place, the call is terminated and a second test call is established, this time from the central test person to the roving test person. The roving tester does not usually try to ascertain the cause of problems, but rather keeps a scoresheet of which telephones function and which do not. To make the tests complete, the roving test person should carry a lineman's test set or telephone instrument equipped with clip leads to perform tests from locations where wiring has been installed but telephone instruments have not yet been installed. The portable test equipment will also be useful in tracing the cause of "no dial tone" by performing tests at intermediate terminal blocks after the initial test survey has been made.

To test additional features of a PBX, such as data transmission capability, the roving test person should have, if possible, a cart equipped with a sample of the data equipment to be used. This will not only permit the tests to be performed at locations where the data equipment is not yet in place, but will also permit a substitution test to be performed at locations where the equipment currently in place appears not to function correctly.

The testing of star-wired rings can be accomplished in a fashion somewhat similar to the PBX tests. A good first test would be to find two stations served by the same wire center and place each in local loop-back modes that test the station itself and then test the path to the wire center. Having established that each station can talk to the wire center, the stations should be placed in operational mode and a station-to-station test should be performed. If this works, one station is chosen as the central test station, and a central test person is assigned to operate it. The roving test person then visits each station associated with the same wire center and places the station in loop-back test mode, establishes its correct operation, and adds it to the ring. As with the PBX, it is probably not necessary to troubleshoot failing stations at this time, but rather to delete them from the ring for later attention. After a wire center has been tested, a similar set of tests is performed for the other wire centers. Finally, a link between two wire centers is enabled and the two tested together, then three, and so on. Manual switches are usually provided in the wire centers to facilitate these tests.

**Testing
a baseband
coaxial cable
system**

A baseband coaxial cable system can be initially tested with a VOM. The test person removes a terminator and tests the resistance between the center conductor of the cable and its shield. The resistance seen should be the sum of the resistances of the center conductor, the distant terminator, the shield, and any intervening connectors. Since the resistance of the distant terminator is known (49.9 ohms for Ethernet), any reading less than that indicates that the cable is shorted. Since the resistance of the center conductor, shield, and intervening connectors should be quite low, a reading more than about a dozen ohms above the terminator resistance indicates an open circuit or loose connection. If the resistances are beyond these bounds, the terminator should be reinstalled and the cable parted at a connector. Now there are two cables, each of which should be tested according to the above rules. This process should be repeated until the failure point is found.

A far more powerful technique, and one highly recommended for networks of more than 100 meters, is the use of a time domain reflectometer (TDR). A TDR looks like an oscilloscope and presents a graphical plot of the voltage on the cable versus time in the same fashion that an oscilloscope would. However, a TDR differs from an oscilloscope in an important way. It applies a short pulse of electrical energy to the cable and displays that pulse and any subsequent pulses that appear on the cable. If the cable has perfectly uniform impedance characteristics, including the terminator at the far end, the pulse applied by the TDR will appear to propagate down a cable of infinite length. If there are any impedance discontinuities, portions of the pulse energy will be reflected at those points and will return to the TDR, where they will be displayed. The magnitude of the reflected pulse will depend on the severity of the impedance discontinuity, and the position of the pulse on the TDR display's time scale will indicate the round-trip time to the point of discontinuity, that is, the location of the fault. Some TDRs are available with devices that record all signals on a moving piece of paper, which resembles adding-machine tape. These devices, called strip chart recorders, are useful for comparing the characteristics of a working network with those of a failing network.

Other network tests, such as ground system tests, are very important, but are beyond the scope of this book. The installation manuals provided by local area network vendors should be consulted for details.

Once the physical channel has been tested, a station should be chosen as the central test station and placed in loop-around mode, where it will apply a signal to the coaxial cable, recover it, and pass the signal through its receiver logic. When this test has been passed for two stations, intercommunication should be attempted. A roving test person, as with the previous network types, then places other stations in loop-around mode and then in operational mode to conduct tests to and from the central test station.

A final word   Since the installation of local area networks can be complex and expensive, it is highly recommended that people purchase the installation guides offered by the vendors whose networks they are considering, and that the quality of these guides and the anticipated level of installation difficulty be considered a factor in network selection.

References   *A Building Planning Guide of Communications Wiring.* Document G320-8059-0. International Business Machines Corporation.
Ethernet Installation Guide. Document EK-ETHER-IN. Digital Equipment Corporation.

Note: Contact your local sales office to obtain ordering information.

6   How things work

All forms of local area network require one or more pieces of electronic hardware to connect terminals, computers, or other devices to the network's transmission medium. For the sake of generality, this chapter will refer to such electronic hardware as "network interface controllers." The operating details of various network interface controllers will be discussed with the objective of comparing their complexity. Since many of the functions involved in interfacing to a network can be accomplished in either hardware or software, the complexity of the network interface controllers will vary not only with the type of local area network being implemented, but also with the hardware/software tradeoffs made by the controller designers.

Methods of attachment to the medium

Figure 32 shows four methods of connecting a network interface controller to a local area network transmission medium. In the first method, commonly used with broadband media, a tap in the main distribution medium creates a stub, which may be several meters long, to which a signal conversion device is attached. The signal conversion device is in turn connected directly to the network interface controller logic, which acts as an interface between the computer or workstation and the local area network.

In the second method, commonly used with baseband media, there is again a tap in the main distribution medium, but the signal conversion device is mounted directly to the main distribution medium by a clamp. The signal conversion device is connected to the network interface controller by a cable which can be several meters long.

In the third method, commonly used in ring networks (without wire centers) and in some baseband bus systems, the main distribution cable is actually brought into the housing of the device containing the network interface controller logic. The signal conversion device is mounted in the distribution cable.

In ring networks that utilize wire centers, or in a PBX, the fourth connection method is used. As in the third method, wiring is brought into the housing of the device containing the network interface controller logic, and the signal conversion device (usually a simple line driver) is mounted therein.

The various technical, topological, and financial benefits to each of these methods are unimportant to this chapter. The purpose of Figure 32 is to indicate that attachment to a network typically involves two components, a signal conversion device and a network interface controller, and that several variations for the physical relationship between these two components exist.

The signal conversion device

Despite the short distances spanned by local area networks, the electrical characteristics of the media used and the possibility of electrical noise pickup preclude the use of conventional logic signaling levels such as would be used within the computers attached to the network.

In local area networks designed to cover a small area, such as a few offices, line drivers and receivers perform adequate signal conditioning and provide adequate noise immunity. Many of these use signaling which meets the requirements of the EIA RS-232-C, RS-422, or RS-423 standards. Simple line drivers, using either RS-422 or a proprietary design, are also used in some PBXs and in some ring networks that use wire centers.

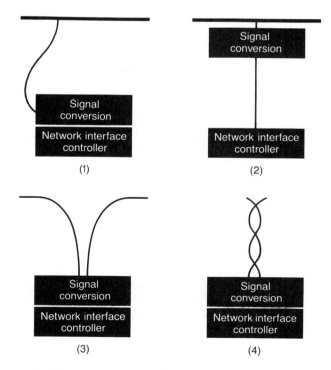

Figure 32. Four ways to attach a network interface controller and a signal conversion device to a transmission medium

Other local area networks, particularly those that operate at speeds above a megabit per second and/or cover a distance of more than a kilometer, utilize more elaborate signaling systems that require "transceivers" or "modems."

The word "transceiver" is a combination of two words (*trans*mitter and re*ceiver*), and is a term commonly used in conjunction with baseband bus systems. The transceivers perform a function similar to that of the line drivers used in smaller, slower systems, but transceivers span greater distances, provide a higher degree of electrical isolation, have improved noise rejection, and are generally more complex and costly.

The word "modem" is also a combination of two words (*mod*ulator and *dem*odulator). Modems differ from transceivers in that they use the digital data being put into them to modify ("modulate") a continuously generated high-frequency signal ("carrier") in a fashion which will enable a modem at the far end of the transmission facility to examine the carrier and determine ("demodulate") what modifications were made, that is, determine what the digital data were. This method is much more complex than simple line drivers, or their somewhat more elaborate cousins, the transceivers, but the use of modulated carriers covers great distances (around the world, if necessary), and is moderately noise immune. Most important, by using different carrier frequencies, multiple transmissions can be put on the same medium.

As should be evident by now, the means of getting digital data onto and off the local area network transmission medium varies widely, from simple line drivers to complex modems. For the purposes of this chapter, we will assume that there is some type of signal conversion device whose function is to convert digital data into a form suitable for transmission over the medium being used, and to convert signals received over the medium back into digital data. For the sake of generality, and to utilize a word which fits into the blocks of diagrams, we will call such a device a modem.

Network interface controller: transmission tasks

The tasks of the network interface controller can be categorized in several ways, but division into transmission tasks and reception tasks is probably the simplest.

Before transmission begins, the network interface controller must perform network access control functions. In a token ring or token bus, the transmission logic must await word from the receiver logic that the token has been received. The token may be withdrawn from the network, or it may be altered into a specific bit pattern which indicates a boundary between two messages, that is, an intermessage spacer or "connector," which is reinserted onto the medium. Transmission begins after the token has been appropriately handled.

In a CSMA/CD system, the transmission logic must await the no-carrier condition (and the expiration of a time-out if a collision occurred on the previous transmission attempt).

Once transmission has begun, the transmitter primarily monitors correct operation. The transmitter's tasks vary with the type of local area network in use. In a token access network, the transmitter's principal task after starting transmission is to place the token at the end of the outgoing message. In some systems, the token is placed immediately at the end of the message, but in others the transmitter waits to confirm correct receipt by the receiving party before relinquishing the token. This latter method is especially applicable to token ring systems that utilize a priority algorithm, as it permits the transmitting station to retain control until it is sure that the transmission has been successful. The drawbacks to this scheme are that some transmission time is wasted, and the "lost token" timers of all stations must be long enough to allow for the additional delay that occurs at the end of the messages.

In a CSMA/CD network, the transmitter's monitoring task begins immediately when transmission starts, as it must check the collision detection lead from the modem to see whether a collision has been detected. If a collision has been detected, the transmitter must transmit a "jamming" pattern for a sufficient period of time to ensure that the other station(s) involved in the collision also detect the collision. Once the jamming signal has been sent, the transmitter must defer for some period of time before attempting to access the medium again. The calculation of the deferral ("backoff") interval may be done in either hardware or software. If it is done in hardware, the mechanism by which it is accomplished should be carefully constructed, as it is absolutely necessary that two nodes, even in a large network, not back off in synchronism, as they will soon encounter sixteen consecutive collisions and abort the transmission. The generation of backoff intervals in software is subject to similar perils and has the added disadvantage of burdening the computer system with calculations. The calculations not only cut down the throughput of the computer, but also may prevent the network interface from making a truly rapid retry, even if the backoff calculation happens to indicate it should, since some amount of time is taken to do the backoff calculation.

A useful additional feature in some CSMA/CD controllers is the ability to detect "late collisions." A collision detection signal which occurs more than the specified maximum round-trip delay after the beginning of transmission indicates either that a station is not waiting for the medium to be idle before transmitting or that the actual round-trip delay is longer than it should be. The first fault is usually caused by a failure in the carrier detect circuitry of a station. The second fault is usually caused by additions to the network that cause it to exceed its proper length.

Finally, the transmitter in any network which has a bus topology should include logic in either the network interface controller or modem to ensure that the transmitter does not get stuck in the ON condition and pollute the medium with endless transmissions.

So far, the discussion of transmission functions has been limited to the tasks associated with placing data onto the transmission medium. The transfer of data into the network interface controller from the computer in which controller is located is of equal importance. These are discussed in the section entitled "DMA Access Methods."

Network interface controller: reception tasks

The network interface control must perform four reception tasks: finding the beginning of a message, address recognition, finding the end of the message, and (in some cases) checking the validity of the message. In addition to these functions, most local area networks require the receiver to perform network operational integrity functions. For example, in a token ring system, the receiver must verify that a token appears periodically. In a token bus scheme, the receiver must verify that the station to which the token was passed has accepted the token and either forwarded it or begun a data transmission. In other systems, the receiver must feed received signals to a comparator during transmission to check that data are getting onto the medium properly and that transmissions from other stations are not interfering.

Finding the beginning of a message

In a CSMA/CD system, there are no signals on the medium when no message is being sent. The no-signaling-during-idle convention is required so that the carrier detect circuit of a station desiring to transmit will properly indicate that the station may commence transmission. When a message begins, the first signals on the line are a special pattern which conditions the receiver clock circuitry for proper reception of the subsequent message data. The special pattern is referred to (in Ethernet) as the "preamble" and consists of a 64-bit alternating 1s and 0s pattern which ends with a double occurrence of 1 to indicate that the destination address is coming next. The reception circuitry recognizes the end of the preamble and treats the appropriate following bits as the address.

In other systems, such as token rings, an idling signal can be sent at all times, since carrier detection is not involved in the access method. This approach keeps the reception clock circuits in a constantly operational state, unless network continuity is broken for some reason. Constant operation of the reception logic allows a receiver to recognize the token when it arrives, at which time the logic treats the appropriate following bits as the address. It is plainly possible to combine the above two schemes. In such a system, the medium would be idle until a token was about to be sent. The token would be preceded by a preamble to condition the receiver clocks, and then the token would be transmitted.

The above descriptions have been a little inexact about the position of the address in the data that follow the preamble and/or token, and have not mentioned address length. The address position and length vary with the local area network being studied, but the topic of address length is worthy of further discussion.

Address length It is common when explaining the concept of addressing to compare its use in computers with its use in telephony. That comparison is particularly apt when discussing local area networks because local area networks use addresses in a number of ways that are analogous to the use of telephone numbers.

Near the beginning of most messages, a field of bits, referred to as the "destination address," designates the computer for which the message is intended. The number of bits required in the destination address field determines how many destinations can be uniquely selected. A field of n bits allows the selection of 2^n unique destinations. Thus, a local area network that has an 8-bit destination address field could have 2^8, or 256, destinations.

In a similar fashion, addresses in a telephone system consist of a field of digits designating for whom the call is intended. In the theoretical case, each digit of a telephone number may have any of ten values (0 through 9) rather than the two values (0,1) allowed in the local area network address case. Thus, an n digit telephone number allows 10^n unique destinations for the call. A telephone system that has two-digit telephone numbers could have 10^2, or 100, uniquely selectable telephone numbers.

Neither a limit of 256 local area network addresses nor a limit of 100 telephone numbers is necessarily a severe problem. In the telephone system case, the solution could be to assign a number or group of numbers (all numbers starting with 0) to an "operator," to whom verbal instructions would be given after dialing, and he or she would access the other telephones in the world. In the local area network case, the solution could be to assign an address or group of addresses to devices that would interpret additional parts of the message to route the message to a destination not directly addressable by the addressing scheme used within the local area network.

The use of very short addresses in a local area network or a telephone system reduces the amount of hardware required and speeds up the use of the network or system by reducing the time spent generating and interpreting addresses. In the local area network case, stations need only receive and store a few bits and compare them with a few bits already stored (the "station address," usually set in switches or a read-only memory) to determine whether or not the message is for that station. In the telephone-system case, short addresses mean fewer digits to be dialed and fewer digits to be stored and interpreted by the switching system. The drawback in both cases is that heavy traffic into and out of the network will swamp the address conversion device in the local area network case and will swamp the operator in the telephone case. Further, in installations where equipment is often moved from one local area network to another, short addresses increase the likelihood that two devices bearing the same address might be placed on the same network. Careful record keeping to prevent such conflicts becomes important.

Special types of addressing

Consider a large corporation which has a department in which there are five people responsible for answering customer questions about computer hardware sold by the corporation. The corporation might choose to set up the telephone system for that department so that a group of four of five lines appeared on everyone's telephone. Dialing a number listed under "Customer Assistance—Hardware" would cause the telephone system to connect through a call to an available line in that group. This arrangement assumes that the caller wants to talk to anyone in that department. In a local area network, a similar arrangement is referred to as a "multicast" address—an address to which any stations of a general class may reply.

Returning to the telephone analogy, let us further assume that as time goes by, customers and friends of the five people also wish to directly select a particular person—they have found that he or she knows the most about a particular type of device or explains things most clearly. In the case of a telephone system, this problem is easily (and rather expensively) solved by giving each individual a personal number. The correct analogy for this situation in the local area network case is a little difficult to describe unless an additional piece of information is known. That piece of information is revealed by the following test: If a person moves from one department to another, does that separate telephone number accompany that person to the new department, or does it stay at the vacated desk to be used by the replacement person? In other words, did people call that number to talk with John Doe because they wanted to talk with him personally or because they wanted to talk with the Customer Assistance person who specialized in communications multiplexers? If the calls were personal, the local area network analogy is that he had a "physical address," that is, an identification of a specific "device"—John Doe. If the calls were based on a specific service he provided (and which his successor will also provide), the telephone number was a "logical address," and calling it expressed a desire to talk to the "person who does *X*."

One other interesting telephone feature would be to have all of the telephones equipped with a "group alerting" feature in which they could all be rung and a building evacuation message given. The local area network analogy of this feature is a "broadcast" message. In present local area network practice, broadcast messages are more common than the multicast messages described previously. The reason for this is that broadcast messages and multicast messages provide a similar capability, with unwanted messages being filtered by software in one case (broadcast) and by hardware in the other case (multicast). Since neither type of message is used frequently, many local area network designers prefer to spend processor time in executing address filtering software rather than implement multicast address recognition capability in the hardware.

Network interface controllers should be able to recognize the various categories of address used in their particular local area network system. As indicated above, these may include broadcast, multicast, logical, and physical. The recognition may be accomplished either in hardware by means of multiway comparator logic or in software. The hardware method requires a moderate amount of logic, but ensures that the comparison process will be done fast enough so that only messages addressed to this station need to be received and stored in a buffer. If the comparison is to be done in software, part of the computational capability of the processor to which the network interface controller is attached must be devoted to this task. Furthermore, if the software is going to take too much time to do the comparison, either the application for which the station is used must limit itself to less addressing flexibility, or else an entire incoming message must be buffered, regardless of destination, until the address comparison algorithm can be executed. This latter approach increases buffering requirements, as messages that have been determined to be addressed to this station must not be destroyed by the need to store other incoming messages while their addresses are examined.

Finding the end of the message

In some CSMA/CD systems—for example, Ethernet—the transmitting station ceases sending carrier upon completing the transmission of the last bit of the cyclic redundancy check that follows the message. A receiving station can detect the cessation of carrier and thus conclude that the previous bits were the cyclic redundancy check.

In a token access system, one method of operation calls for a station desiring to transmit to find the token, alter it to form another special pattern called a "connector," affix the message it desires to send, and then append the token (either immediately or after a delay to confirm correct reception). Thus, a receiver can determine the end of the message by receipt of the token, receipt of a connector, or receipt of some other data pattern identified to be "end of message."

*Checking
the validity
of the message*

The customary way of determining the validity of a message is for a receiver to perform a mathematical operation upon the incoming data (calculate a cyclic redundancy check, or CRC) and compare the results of that calculation with the calculation results sent by the transmitting station at the end of the message. Depending upon how the comparison is done and the type of local area network, the desired result may be all zeros or some predetermined value.

CRC calculation can be performed in hardware or in software. A particular CRC calculation that produces a 32-bit result has been rarely found to improperly indicate that a complexly altered message is correct. This CRC calculation can be implemented as a single LSI (large scale integrated) part, so the logic to do CRC in hardware is not substantial. The alternative, software calculation via exclusive-OR instructions and tables, places a considerable burden on the processor to which the network interface controller is attached.

While designers of bus networks usually feel that CRC checking is a necessity, designers of some networks utilizing point-to-point links believe that their transmission systems have sufficiently low error rates that CRC hardware can be eliminated and a simpler parity and/or format checking scheme used instead. Errors that escape the simplified checking are dealt with by higher-level software. This does not mean that the higher-level software calculates CRC; rather, it treats all messages as good and relies on other mechanisms to detect faults. Faults are assumed to be rare enough that the complex processes needed to deal with them are not invoked often enough to justify the cost of complete lower-level error detection in hardware or software. No additional software is required by this approach, as the ability of higher-level software to detect errors is required regardless of whether or not the local area network has CRC hardware.

Flow control

Ring networks have the unique opportunity to implement flow control at a very low level—that is, with minimal software intervention by the source or destination stations. This is accomplished in some systems by having a "refuse" bit near the end of the message. The hardware at the receiving station leaves this bit set if it has insufficient buffers to handle the message at this time or if it detects errors in the message or format. The transmitting station can then wait some period of time and try again. The transmitting station hardware does not acknowledge to its associated software that the transmission has taken place until a message circulates without refusal by the destination station.

The above system eliminates the need for message numbering for flow control purposes, although message numbering for error control purposes would still be desirable. The reason for this is that a ring allows the sending station to receive a message after it has circulated past the recipient and thus can confirm correct reception. However, if an error has occurred, the sending station does not know whether the error occurred while the message was on its way to the recipient or on the way back. Thus, the sender does not know whether or not the recipient has a correct copy. Since retransmission may be required, message numbering is essential.

Other networks can only perform flow control at a higher level. In Ethernet, for example, the only way reception hardware can refuse a message is to "drop it into the bit bucket." If the software has independently numbered the messages before giving them to the network controller, the software can always request retransmission of any messages which are not acknowledged. Many designers of simple interfaces for personal computers rely on retransmission to solve the problem of momentary overloads in such interfaces.

The practice of dropping messages to deal with overload conditions in small computers is not good, because it can cause substantial performance degradation in the station that is transmitting, which may be a large host. The reason for host performance degradation is that the transmitting station hardware assumes successful transmission as soon as a message has been placed on the medium without encountering collision. The network interface hardware tells the network interface driver (software) that the transmission was "successful," and the network interface driver directs the network interface hardware to send the next message (which may be to a different destination). The network interface driver retains a copy of the message in case a transmission error or other problem requires retransmission. The driver also starts a timer awaiting an acknowledgment from the message recipient. At some point, that timer expires because the message was discarded by the recipient. The driver must then determine where in host memory the copy of the message is, and queue it up for retransmission. This task is not trivial and can degrade the performance of the host, especially if it occurs frequently.

It is highly desirable for a local area network to have a flow control mechanism, or for the interfaces to have sufficient buffering and processing capability so that a very low percentage (5 percent or less) of messages is discarded because of congestion.

DMA access methods

So far, this chapter has worked its way from the transmission medium, through the signal conversion system, and through the transmission and reception logic. It is now time to discuss where transmitted characters come from, and where received characters go.

DMA, or direct memory access, refers to a data transfer system in which a device accesses the memory in a computer system for the purpose of directly reading or writing data from or to that memory. Typically, a program running in the computer takes no active part in these data transfers other than to specify a starting address in memory and the number of transfers to take place. An alternative method, "Programmed I/O," differs in that the program transfers the data by means of "move" instructions, typically performing one such instruction for each word transferred. DMA transfers operate considerably faster than programmed transfers, but require more hardware, since bus control logic, address registers, and transfer counters are required.

While DMA logic can theoretically operate at the maximum transfer speed of whatever bus connects the logic to the memory, other devices such as the processor, disks, tapes, or other network interfaces typically share that bus and/or that memory. Therefore, depending upon the configuration of the computer system upon which the network interface is located, one cannot assume that the bus and/or memory will always be available when the DMA logic in the network interface wants it. At the very least, one should assume that the processor is using the memory 50 percent of the time.

There is one way to guarantee that the memory is available to the DMA logic in the network interface at all times when the processor is not using the memory, and that is to place the network interface "first on the bus" and design it to operate in "bus hog" mode; that is, once it has access to the bus, it keeps the bus until the transfers are completed. This design approach is often used with disks and tapes, since they must move physical media into position and then have bus access immediately. Needless to say, not all devices in a computer system can be "first on the bus," and "bus hog" mode can cause "data late" errors on devices to which bus access was denied by a "hog" further up the bus. It is therefore wise to design interfaces with some amount of buffering so that they can afford to wait for bus access and to design their DMA logic to periodically relinquish the bus and allow others access. It might even be desirable to limit the amount of time between bus accesses, so that two devices which merely relinquish access do not take alternate turns and "freeze out" other devices. The above discussion is best summarized as follows:

1. DMA gives superior performance to programmed I/O.
2. DMA devices should be designed to not require being first on the bus and to relinquish the bus between transfers. These requirements can be waived only if the system on which the network interface is to be installed will not have disks, tapes, or another network interface.

Buffering requirements in DMA interfaces

If a network interface has DMA logic designed to the "good citizenship" requirements of item 2 above, it must be designed with sufficient buffering to withstand being denied access to the bus for some period of time. The design of the transmitter logic is the simpler case and will be considered first.

If the transmitter were equipped with a buffer capable of storing an entire packet,* the DMA system could load that buffer from the main memory and then transmission could be initiated. Since the transmitter need not start transmission until the packet buffer has been loaded, bus access is not particularly time critical, unless it is very important that the interface be able to send back-to-back packets.

If the transmitter had two buffers, each capable of storing a packet, the second buffer could be prepared, that is, loaded from main memory, during transmission from the first buffer. The capability of transmitting from alternate buffers would permit the transmission of back-to-back packets. Depending upon the rules used in the local area network being considered, the ability to transmit back-to-back packets may or may not be necessary or desirable.

Reception poses more stringent requirements on interface design than does transmission. Earlier in this chapter, it was explained that dropping packets was undesirable because of the performance implications at the station doing the transmission. We might add that dropping packets also wastes the time of other stations that are awaiting access to the medium; the medium is being used to transmit data that are being discarded. With these thoughts in mind, the question of achieving adequate buffering in the receiver section of an interface arises.

Buffers are areas into which data arriving at rate λ_{in} are deposited in preparation for withdrawal at rate λ_{out}. While the withdrawal rate must equal the arrival rate in the long term, the rates may vary in the short term if the magnitude of their variation and the length of time during which the variation takes place are not too great. In the case of a network interface, the worst case arises when a long packet is being transfered from a receive buffer to main memory while a succession of short packets is also arriving, and the network transfer rate is much higher than the DMA transfer rate. An example utilizing Ethernet packets follows.

The maximum length of the data portion of an Ethernet packet is 1500 bytes. Assuming that these bytes are being transferred over a 16-bit bus at a rate of one 2-byte transfer every microsecond, this process will take 750 microseconds. The minimum length of the data portion of an Ethernet packet is 46 bytes, but there are 8 bytes of preamble, 14 bytes of header, and 4 bytes of CRC. The minimum packet size is therefore 72 bytes, which is 576 bits and should take 57.6 microseconds to transmit. However, a 9.6 microsecond interpacket gap is also

---

*In most of this book, the term "message" is used to refer to any communication between two points in a network. Most local area networks use packet switching, where transmission of a message requires the transmission of one or more packets, each of which is a single entity of limited length prefixed by addressing information and often followed by an error-checking code. Since hardware requirements are now being discussed, the exact term for a transmission unit, "packet," is used in this section.

required, so the total transmission time of the minimum packet would be 67.2 microseconds. Therefore, during the 750 microseconds that it takes to transfer the maximum-length packet into main memory, eleven (750/67.2 = 11) minimum-length packets could arrive.

While the above calculations are specific to a 10-Mbps Ethernet and a 16-bit processor bus, and postulate the highly unlikely case of a maximum-length packet immediately followed by 11 consecutive minimum-length packets, designers and purchasers of local area network interfaces should make calculations of this type to see what the worst-case numbers are, and make similar calculations for cases which they consider likely. It might also be a useful exercise to test the sensitivity of a design to various changes. For example, what if the internal bus were 8 bits? 32 bits? What if the system were so busy that transfers only could be accomplished once every 3 microseconds?

It should also be noted that during the 750 microseconds it took for the DMA transfer in the above example, a single packet of more than 900 bytes could have arrived, rather than 11 packets of 72 bytes each. A buffering system which can only handle one large packet is useless in the many-small-packets case, and a buffering system which can handle 11 packets of maximum size is wasteful. Rather, a buffering system that can dynamically deal with received packets of varying lengths would be very useful.

Interfaces between the DMA system and the software

There are several ways of arranging buffers so that a program can manage them conveniently and a microprocessor in a network interface controller can progress from buffer to buffer without pause. One method is to alternate between two buffers—a "primary buffer" and an "alternate buffer." A transmission program, for example, loads a packet into each buffer and tells the microprocessor which one to start with. The microprocessor completes transmission from one buffer and proceeds to the other, generating an interrupt. The program now knows that it is safe to replace the packet in the first buffer and establish a new byte count for that buffer. When the microprocessor finishes sending from the second buffer, it returns to the first, generating an interrupt. This process continues until there are no more packets to send.

Another method of sending from (or receiving into) successive buffers involves the use of linked lists. In a linked list, blocks of memory are set aside for "linked list headers." A linked list header contains four pieces of information:

1. The address of the next header
2. The address of the packet buffer
3. The size of the packet buffer
4. Control bits indicating special actions to be taken before or during the transmission of the packet

When the microprocessor begins transmission of a packet buffer, it picks up these four pieces of information and stores them in its memory. When the first packet buffer has been completed, it uses the "address of next header" information to find the next header and repeat the process. If the "address of next header" is zero, the end of the list of buffers has been reached, and there are no more packets to send.

Yet another method is the use of ring buffers. In the ring buffer system, a block of memory is set aside containing (for example) eight of the headers listed above. However, the "address of next header" is replaced with a status bit that is 1 if the microprocessor has not "picked up" the buffer information, and 0 if it has. Thus the microprocessor rotates through the header blocks, taking the information and acknowledging receipt of that information by changing status bits from 1 to 0. The computer program, managing the buffers, checks the status bits for changes from 1 to 0 and installs new headers on discovering 0s.

While the linked list and ring systems were described above in terms of transmission, a symmetrical approach can be used to handle multiple reception buffers.

Summary

Computers attach to local area network transmission media via signal conversion devices and network interface controllers. Whereas signal conversion devices are relatively straightforward, network interface controllers typically reflect a wide range of design choices. Designers or purchasers of local area networks need to be aware of those design choices and need to assign costs. Determining hardware costs is simple, but these are often minimized by shifting a processing burden onto the software, both in the device in which the interface is located and in other devices that are communicating with the interface. The methods of doing address comparison, multicast address comparison, CRC calculation, backoff calculation, and the buffering capabilities all influence processing overhead. The discussions in this chapter are not intended to imply that one should use or buy maximal quantities of hardware, but they do imply that one should analyze the processing overhead required for various schemes, determine what percent of the processor that overhead will require, and take that percentage of the processor's cost as part of the cost of interfacing to the network. Only in this way can the true cost of the hardware and processor time to interface to the network be determined.

7 Operations and maintenance

In many ways the use of a local area network is like the use of another shared resource—the electric system. Users gain the benefits of economy of scale, and they gain the benefit of not having to run their own generators, use candles, or otherwise try to heat and light their homes independently. Like the electric system, however, users of local area networks require that the economy, availability, and reliability of the shared system meet certain standards, or else they are better off being independent.

Several other chapters have mentioned items related to economy. Topology, access methods, media, installation factors, and interface design all influence economy. These items also influence availability and reliability, concepts which are an important ingredient in the operation and maintenance of local area networks, and hence key concepts for discussion in this chapter.

Availability

Simply stated, availability is a measure of how often a system is available at the time a user wants to use it. A system which is never down has 100 percent availability. In practice, computer systems do fail, preventive maintenance is required, and system reconfigurations requiring down time are made. A simple formula for determining availability on a weekly basis would be as follows:

$$\frac{168 - (\text{\# failures} \times \text{MTTR}) - \text{PM} - \text{RT}}{168} \times 100\%$$

168 = number of hours in a week

\# failures = number of failures

MTTR = mean time to repair a failure

PM = time spent on preventive maintenance

RT = time spent on reconfiguration

Unfortunately, the formula given is appropriate only for a single-user system. Availability of a multiuser system is far more complex, as failure of a user's system, failure of the network, or failure of computers which provide services the user needs are all part of the calculation. Each of these other elements is represented by a similar equation and the equations are combined in a fashion that represents the possible failure conditions. Despite the complexity of creating an appropriate equation, increasing availability is accomplished by reducing the size of the terms that are subtracted from 168 in the numerator of the equation.

Number of failures

The number of failures encountered is primarily a function of the size of the network and the environmental conditions. Failure rates for electronic components under several categories of environmental condition can be predicted. The more components a device has, and the further it is from moderate temperature and humidity conditions, the more likely it is to fail.

A strict calculation on the basis of Military Standard 217, an often used source of component failure predictions, would suggest that all redundant circuits and maintenance aids should be eliminated to keep the component count down. Keeping the component count down would keep the failure rate down. This is unwise for two reasons:

1. In many designs it is possible to utilize redundant circuits so that the failure of a component does not interfere with system operation at all, thus taking the component failure out of the "# of failures" term entirely. Replacement of the component moves into the "preventive maintenance" category, but may be able to be accomplished without interrupting operations.
2. Lack of maintenance aids greatly increases the MTTR (mean time to repair) multiplier.

In some local area network designs, momentary failures occur when stations are added to or removed from the network. For example, in a token ring equipped with bypass relays, the relays can take a hundred milliseconds to function (contact operation and bounce time). During that time, the token will get lost and token recovery procedures will come into play. This is not necessarily a serious problem, but could become a problem in a large system if users turned their computers off and on frequently. In a bus system, the addition of transceivers or modems may bring the system to a halt if the transceiver or modem design requires severing the cable or removing terminators.

**Mean time
to repair**

MTTR has always been an important aspect of computer system design, but becomes crucial in local area networks, owing to their physically dispersed nature. Without good maintenance aids, strong legs become a job requirement for network technicians.

Wire center token rings and PBXs should, in theory, have good MTTR characteristics, since a technician at a wire center or PBX has access to the wiring for each station and can isolate it from the rest of the network to perform tests. If the station has the capability of performing a self-test without using the station wiring, and then a self-test using the station wiring, rapid fault isolation should be possible.

**Preventive
maintenance**

Preventive maintenance generally includes such tasks as cleaning air filters, lubricating bearings, and checking adjustments on mechanical devices. In a local area network, performing these tasks at user stations should not interrupt network operations, and thus the time spent should not appear in the formula shown earlier. It might be wise for a prospective network purchaser to check this point, however. Performing preventive maintenance at a server may require network down time, or at least lack of that service. Scheduling such maintenance for off-peak hours is one possible way of making the lack of availability acceptable to the users. One should note, however, that "off-peak" may be midnight or 7 A.M., depending on whether the network is installed in a business or a university. A more sophisticated system that "shadowed" the files on the file server or provided a backup printer would permit preventive maintenance to occur at any time, and would also protect against down time due to failures. Such duplicated servers thus improve two of the terms in the availability formula, but at considerable cost.

While the cleaning and lubrication of mechanical devices should not be postponed, many electronic devices are best cared for by the rule "If it ain't broke, don't fix it." Such a philosophy requires a method of determining when things are "broke." Better yet would be a method of determining when things are about to break, as then the network users would not be inconvenienced by an actual failure, and preventive maintenance (sometimes called "causal maintenance" when it causes a failure) would only be applied when necessary. Determining the "about to break" condition is the role of maintenance aids and network statistics.

**Maintenance aids
and network
statistics**

A local area network "breaks" when an open circuit or short circuit occurs in the transmission medium, when a network controller malfunctions, or when the network is overloaded.

Open circuits

In a wire-center token ring utilizing bypass relays, an open circuit within a wire center is unlikely, although a faulty bypass relay could cause such a failure. More likely, the wiring to a station has been broken. Such a break puts the bypass relay in bypass mode, and network operation continues. Maintenance personnel detect the altered state of the relay and check the station line continuity using a volt-ohm-meter, a time domain reflectometer, or visual inspection.

In a CSMA/CD bus system, an open circuit in a transceiver cable could cause lack of received data (and lack of carrier detection). The interface controller would transmit any time it wished, but upon starting transmission would notice that it could not hear itself and would shut down, having detected the lack of received signal. An open circuit in the transmit pair would create a condition where the interface controller could hear other transmissions but not its own, an easily detectable and analyzable fault. To detect an open circuit in the collision detection pair, a transceiver can generate a flash of collision detect at the end of a transmission to verify that the collision detection circuit and wiring are working. If the network interface controller has been designed to look for this signal, and does not see it, the controller would shut down and report the error.

In a CSMA/CD bus system, an open circuit in a coaxial cable would create an impedance discontinuity which would cause signal reflections that caused the number of collisions to rise sharply. CSMA/CD network interface controllers should keep track of the number of transmission attempts which resulted in no collision, one collision, two collisions, and sixteen collisions. A rise in those statistics could indicate a cable fault. In addition, the higher levels of software could be arranged to send error messages to their system consoles, or otherwise indicate their inability to access other stations. Finding the open circuit on a CSMA/CD bus system would be best accomplished by using a time domain reflectometer.

In a non-wire-center token ring, or a token bus, an open circuit would cause the token to disappear. Token regeneration procedures would be invoked, but would not succeed owing to the open circuit. Interface controllers would be designed to give an error message to the software when the token regeneration procedures fail. In addition, the higher levels of software would complain about inability to reach other stations. Finding the open circuit would be best accomplished by using a time domain reflectometer.

In a PBX, an open circuit is most likely to occur in the station wiring and will be exhibited to the user as an inability to obtain dial tone. Service personnel can test at intermediate terminal blocks until dial tone in obtained, and then search for the discontinuity using a volt-ohm-meter, a time domain reflectometer, or visual inspection.

It is also very important in ring systems that the addition of new stations not cause an open circuit. This can occur if the added station were nonfunctional. A complete set of off-line tests adequate to ensure proper operation is required before the station is added to the ring.

Short circuits

In a wire center token ring, a short circuit within a wire center is unlikely. More likely, the wiring to a station has been shorted. Such a short puts the bypass relay in bypass mode, and troubleshooting is similar to that for an open circuit (see above).

In a CSMA/CD system, a short circuit in a transceiver cable or coaxial cable would cause failures similar to those created by an open circuit (see above).

In a non-wire-center token ring, or a token bus, a short circuit would produce token loss in a fashion similar to an open circuit (see above).

In a PBX, a short circuit is most likely to occur in the station wiring, and will be exhibited to the user as an inability to obtain dial tone and in the equipment as a permanent off-hook condition. Service personnel can test loop resistance from the PBX or break the station loop, test at intermediate terminal blocks until proper operation is obtained, and then search for the short using a volt-ohm-meter, a time domain reflectometer, or visual inspection.

Controller malfunction

In a token ring system, the most common controller malfunction is dropping the token. To detect this occurrence, some systems rely on a central station to check for periodic appearance of the token. Other systems rely on each station to monitor the medium for message flags and tokens. In either case, once the loss of the token is detected, a new one is generated.

As indicated above, it is possible for the carrier detect circuitry in a CSMA/CD system to fail because of open circuits, short circuits, or failed components. If it fails in the ON condition, the network interface controller will never transmit, believing that someone else is transmitting. A time-out in hardware or software to detect this condition must be provided. If the carrier detect circuitry fails in the OFF condition, the station will transmit whenever it has something to send, perhaps creating a collision. However, this condition can be detected by noticing that the network interface controller cannot hear itself. The controller should shut down and report the error under these conditions.

Another possible failure in a CSMA/CD controller occurs in the collision detection system. As indicated above, to detect this, a transceiver can generate a flash of collision detect at the end of a transmission to verify that the collision detection circuit is working. Network interface controllers designed according to IEEE 802.3 and Ethernet 2.0 specifications are designed to look for this signal, and if they do not see it, the controllers will shut down and report the error.

Another feature useful in CSMA/CD applications is the "late collision" detector. A collision which occurs more than one round-trip time after transmission initiation indicates that some station is not performing its carrier detection check properly, or else that the network has a longer round-trip delay than it should.

In both CSMA/CD and token systems, a useful mechanism for testing controller operation is the "hello message." In such a message, a station desiring to conduct a test transmits a special message to a destination. The destination, recognizing that this is a test message, interchanges the source and destination address fields, and sends it back. In this way, a testing station can check for the proper operation of all other stations. Any station can perform the role of testing station.

One word of caution is in order with regard to maintenance features such as the "hello message." Systems designed to support such features must provide adequate protection against those who might use the maintenance functions for malicious or mischievous purposes. For example, a malicious person who fired a stream of "hello messages" at a large host could greatly inhibit the operation of that host unless the hardware and software therein limited the buffer resources and response time allocated to such messages.

Any discussion of controller failure must include PBXs, as the simple wiring associated with PBXs often leads people to assume that PBXs are simple. Looking inside the switching system box(es) will reveal that the controller logic is quite complex. PBX controller designers face a tradeoff between minimizing the number of circuit cards in the controller by putting many things on one card, and minimizing the disruption caused when a card must be replaced by putting only a few things on a card. Traditionally, PBX designers have limited the amount of functionality on a single card and provided several units that perform the same function, so that failures cause a degradation of traffic handling capability rather than actual service disruption.

PBX software should include test routines that exercise the equipment during periods of low traffic, and should include time-out routines that isolate and identify portions of the controller that are not functioning correctly.

Network overload

The performance of various local area networks is the subject of much controversy because the number of bits in the average message, the balance of traffic among the stations, the size of bit buffers in token ring stations, and other factors will influence the results obtained in statistical analysis.

A possible approach to comparing token rings and CSMA/CD buses is to consider the inefficiencies of each rather than their virtues. For example, in a token ring or bus, time is wasted waiting for the token to traverse the ring or bus and arrive at the station desiring to transmit. On the average, the token will be on the opposite side of the ring (halfway through the address list in a bus system) from the station desiring to transmit. That is neither the worst case (the token just passed) nor the best case (the token is about to arrive). In a CSMA/CD system, time is wasted when a collision occurs.

If we look at where the two systems waste time, we can deduce that

CSMA/CD systems are most efficient when there are no collisions (i.e., light load), as they are instantly ready for transmission to occur. Token systems are most efficient when the token is not traversing a ring (or address list) past stations that don't want to transmit, but rather is busily going from active station to active station.

The performance of CSMA and token ring networks is compared in Figure 33, which was sketched from several charts presented in the references. The vertical axis is the packet transfer time, and the horizontal axis is the throughput rate divided by the transmission rate of the medium, a measure of loading.

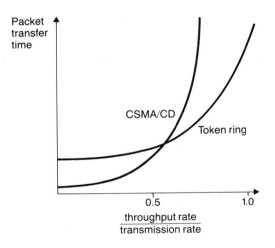

Figure 33. Performance of token rings and CSMA/CD

As indicated in the chart, the delays in CSMA/CD become severe at about 50 percent loading. In token rings, the delays are much higher than CSMA/CD at low loading, but do not rise sharply.

To appraise network performance, a token ring network interface controller might wish to record the amount of time it spends waiting for a token. The timing (but not the recording) is already required for purposes of detecting a lost token.

As indicated in the figure, CSMA/CD networks provide excellent performance at low load levels, but degrade rapidly in high traffic conditions. Assuming that the traffic on most networks will grow gradually as more stations are added, it would be wise for CSMA/CD network interface controllers to keep track of the number of transmission attempts which resulted in no collision, one collision, two collisions, and sixteen collisions. Numbers of collisions between two and sixteen could also be counted, if desired. These statistics would help determine when the CSMA/CD network was in danger of becoming overloaded.

Overloads in PBXs are usually indicated by lack of dial tone or the receipt of a fast busy tone (all trunks busy). Even if the network is nonblocking, the processing of calls may be delayed in periods of heavy traffic. The PBX should be provided with traffic counters that indicate the number of calls attempted, the number blocked by lack of dial tone (if applicable), the number of times certain services (including trunks to other systems) were unavailable, and the number of users attempting to use the services that were blocked. It would also be useful to know the number of times dial tone was late by more than three seconds.

Reconfiguration   Users of timesharing systems are all too familiar with the system message "SYSTEM WILL BE UNAVAILABLE 6 PM TO 9 PM WHILE SERVICE ADDS 16 MORE TERMINAL LINES." The need to turn off power while adding components, the need to change cabling arrangements, and the need to tell the system software about the new components typically combine to require the users to wait several hours while the system is reconfigured.

Local area networks solve many of these problems. PBXs have always been designed for reconfiguration with the power on; the primary reconfiguration tasks are simply running wire and updating the switching program to turn on the new service. Only the program update endangers the system operation, and even that is often replicated so that one copy is updated at a time. Wire-center token rings can be installed with unused connections bridged by bypass relays. An additional station, or another wire center, can be added and checked out before the momentary interruption caused by opening the bypass relay takes place. Ethernet systems utilizing "penetration taps" (sometimes called "vampire taps") can have stations added with, if any, only momentary interruption, as the transceiver associated with the new station is connected to the coaxial cable. The station can perform a stand-alone checkout before being added to the system. Broadband systems can be wired with terminated drops to every office at relatively little expense, and new stations added by replacing a terminator with a modem. Addition of taps and splitters to add more stations is a complex matter, however.

In summary, the physical aspects of reconfiguration in most local area networks are such that network operation is either unaffected or only modestly affected by reconfiguration. The addition of new stations and new services may have software impact that affects network operation, however, just as "regenerating" the system was required in timesharing systems. Worst case, the additions may require that stations be "rebooted."

Booting stations in a local area network

Booting is the process of giving a computer system enough intelligence—that is, loading enough program—so that the system can load additional programs that will permit it to perform its intended application. The program to accomplish this usually exists in a read only memory (ROM) in the computer system, and the reading of this ROM is initiated in response to the detection of a command to do so arriving over the network, or in response to the detection of an abnormality such as power failure.

A very simple computer system whose tasks were controlled by a program (in which its programmers had great confidence) could have both its boot program and its operating program in ROM, but this is rarely the case. More frequently, the boot program initiates a read request to some other storage medium to obtain the program information necessary to restore the computer system to full functionality. A cassette or similar tape located in the computer system is one possibility. If the system is equipped with a floppy or other type of disk, the program may be loaded from that medium. Local area networks provide a third alternative—the ability to obtain the operating program over the network.

The ability of stations on a local area network to obtain program loads over the network saves time, because the transfer rate of a disk on a file server sending a file over a network is usually greater than that of a local cassette. Program loading via a network saves money, because cassettes and floppies may be unnecessary on some systems that required them only for program loading. Program loading via a network also solves revision control problems and system configuration updating problems by providing a single master copy of software that is kept up to date. In large systems, it would be advisable to calculate the amount of time it takes the network to perform program loading, however. During electrical storms or other power line disturbances, a network which relied heavily on down-line program loading might be useless for substantial periods of time.

Despite the advantages of program loading via a network, there is one class of program which should be stored or loadable locally, and that is the diagnostic. Regardless of the type of local area network being used, there are types of station malfunction which prohibit that station from being connected to the network until the problem is found and corrected. Since such stations cannot be connected until they are repaired, diagnosis must proceed without network connection. This may mean that a portable local load device is required, that a separate serial line connection must be provided, or that on-board ROM diagnostics must be capable of finding network-threatening faults.

Documentation

Proper documentation is important both in reduced MTTR and in preventing failures. The physical location of all cables, connection boxes, wire centers, stations, gateways, modems, and so on, must be thoroughly documented at the time of installation, and these records must be kept absolutely up to date. It is wise to assign one person the task of maintaining the records of the physical medium, to keep those records in that person's office, and to allow only that person to make changes to the medium. These records would be useful for troubleshooting, network expansion, and protection against service interruptions caused by unauthorized or accidental movement of cables.

A higher-level set of records should be maintained that not only duplicates the location information for servers, gateways, and stations (neglecting cabling details), but also lists the type of equipment, network addressing, software in use, and the like. These records should be handled by a network manager, whose tasks are to assist in troubleshooting, to plan network changes, and to assign addresses.

Reliability

As indicated in the discussion of availability, reliability is a measure of how infrequently something fails. A device which never fails is 100 percent reliable. Although no device is 100 percent reliable, simplicity, careful design (which may include redundancy), and good environment can be strong positive factors in achieving reliability.

Of these three factors, simplicity may have to be the one most quickly traded away. As was discussed in Chapter 6, achieving high performance usually requires an investment in hardware, that is, abandoning simplicity to obtain performance. Redundant circuitry and maintenance aids reduce the liklihood of service interruption and decrease its duration when it occurs, but they increase the complexity of the design.

The second factor in creating a reliable system, careful design, is difficult to analyze without the circuit schematics and a trained designer to assist in the analysis. If these are available, a prospective purchaser should by all means use them. Recommendations from users who already have the equipment installed may also be helpful.

Finally, the provision of a good environment for the network equipment is a factor over which network purchasers, managers, and users do have some control. For example, PBXs have in the past often been located in hot, wet, cramped quarters in the basements of buildings. The reliability of such systems has reflected their surroundings—poor. Furthermore, the cramped quarters and poor lighting have contributed to a high MTTR. Computers, such as those used for gateways, servers, and terminal concentrators, have rarely been so mistreated, but the trend toward wider operating temperature tolerance and smaller packaging sometimes tempts network managers to place these items in broom closets and under desks. Network apparatus does not generally require separate rooms with raised floors and high-quality air conditioning, but neither should it be abused.

An important factor in reliability is designing systems and placing apparatus so that things are touched as little as possible. Anyone who has ever worked for a computer company and visited customer sites knows that some customers say, "That's a great computer. We leave it in that room running day and night and never touch it." Other customers say, "That computer is a lemon. We use it here in the lab and every time we reconfigure it, something breaks." The moral is simple—computers run best when they're left alone.

Summary

Local area networks are only valuable if they are available and reliable. To achieve these goals, the hardware and software used must be simple, but with robustness and ease of maintenance built into the design. The network must not only be easy to repair once it malfunctions, but also be easy to analyze during normal operation to assess its performance and "state of health." Maintenance aids, network monitoring provisions, good documentation, and careful attention to environmental factors are all required for the successful operation and maintenance of local area networks.

References

Bux, Werner. "Local-area Subnetworks: A Performance Comparison," in *Local Networks for Computer Communications*, Proceedings of IFIP WG6.4 International Workshop on Local Networks, Zurich, August 1980, North Holland Books.

Davies, D. W., et al. *Computer Networks and Their Protocols*. New York: John Wiley & Sons, 1979.

Flint, David C. *The Data Ring Main*. New York: John Wiley & Sons, 1983.

Marathe, Madhav, and Hawe, Bill. "Predicting Ethernet Capacity—A Case Study," Proceedings of the Computer Performance Evaluation Users Group, Washington, D.C., October 1982.

8   Protocols

The tasks of a data communication system include delivery of information that is correct, in proper time sequential order, and understandable by the recipient. To accomplish these functions, electrical circuits, error-detection systems, error-correction systems, information coding, data flow control, data formating systems, and other hardware/software subsystems must all perform in a cooperative fashion following a set of rules, or protocols.

Dictionaries define "protocol" as being the set of rules and ceremonies by which diplomats and heads of state communicate. The rules of diplomatic protocol ensure that communications are completely and correctly understood by both parties. In data communication, protocols perform a similar function, and their use is almost as complex as the use of diplomatic protocols.

As indicated above, many functions must be performed to accomplish the task of data communication, and there is generally a protocol for each of these functions. A complete family of protocols is necessary to do the complete job. To assist people in designing protocol families, the International Organization for Standardization (ISO) has developed a model in which each protocol that makes up the family is a "layer" that performs certain functions for the protocol (layer) above it. The ISO model, it should be emphasized, does not specify the exact details of each protocol;* rather, it specifies a *way of designing protocol families*, that is, what layers should be present and what functions each layer should perform. Two protocol families that are "ISO-compatible" cannot necessarily intercommunicate. Furthermore, many protocol families follow the ISO model only very loosely.

The idea that protocols are arranged as layers is a bit difficult to grasp, but anyone who has ever sent a letter has used layered protocols without realizing it. In writing a letter, it is customary (i.e., according to protocol) to acknowledge receipt of previous correspondence

---

*Although the ISO model does not specify individual protocols, the ISO organization does specify and approve protocols.

and then to discuss whatever topics one chooses. The text of the letter is preceded by a greeting ("Dear John") and concluded with a closing ("Sincerely"), followed by a signature. The completed letter is then packaged according to postal regulations (another protocol) and sent to the post office. Note that there was a protocol for what was in the text, a protocol for framing the text between a greeting and closing, and a protocol for physically transporting it. Figure 34 shows these three protocols in block diagram form.

An important part of the concept of layered protocols is the idea that each layer provides a service for the layers above it. In the letter-

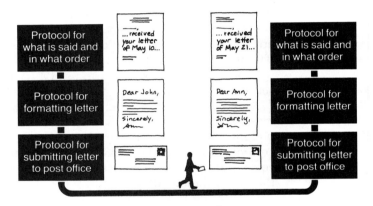

Figure 34. Postal service protocols

writing example, the post office provides a letter-delivery service, and the postal protocol ensures the rapid and economical delivery of the correct letter to the correct party by specifying envelope sizes that fit the sorting machines and by specifying address formats that can be machine read or conveniently read by humans.

The formatting protocol specifying a greeting and closing ensures that the message is for the intended party and verifies the identity of the sender. If you receive a letter that begins "Dear John" and your name is Larry, you know that the sender placed the wrong letter in the envelope. Similarly, receiving a letter with a stranger's signature may indicate that something has gone wrong.

The "protocol for what is said and in what order" guides both the message sender and the message recipient. For example, specifying that previous correspondence be acknowledged ensures that the two correspondents realize when a message is lost. If the letter begins, "Received yours of March 7," and the recipient knows he or she sent another letter on March 20, there is reason to suspect that a letter is missing.

The layering of protocols permits services to be substituted with minimal impact. For example, the correspondents might prefer to have their letters delivered by an overnight package delivery service rather than the post office. Figure 35 would then apply.

Figure 35 differs from Figure 34 only at the lowest level. The typical differences are the type of envelope used, the pickup and delivery

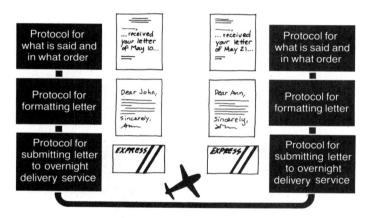

Figure 35. Overnight delivery service protocols

points, and the rate paid. The higher-level protocols remain unchanged. One may presume that any overnight service which required its customers to change some higher-level protocol, such as the message format or content, would not have very many customers.

Several layers of protocol might be altered if the substitution of services occurred at a higher level, however. Consider the case of a telephone call, as shown in Figure 36.

The "protocol for operating a telephone" (getting dial tone and dialing the desired number) permits the telephone company to provide a prompt and accurate connection service between the parties wishing to communicate. As with the post office, access to a service point (mailbox/telephone) is required, an address is required, and a service charge is collected.

Once the connection has been established, the "protocol for a telephone call" provides identification via an exchange of greetings ("Jane Doe speaking;" "Hello, this is Frank"). This is followed by conversation, and the call concludes with an exchange of goodbyes indicating the imminent breaking of the connection.

The top level of communications, the "protocol for what is said and in what order," is often unchanged between a telephone call and a letter, at least in terms of the broad outline of acknowledging previous correspondence and announcing the reason for or subject of this correspondence.

Figure 36. Telephone call protocols

In summary, even such everyday correspondence as letters and telephone calls follows a layered protocol format. The layers provide an ordering of services that makes the correspondence more accurate and easy to understand. Furthermore, the layering allows for the substitution of services if special circumstances demand it ("This has to be there overnight" or "I must communicate right now").

Data communication protocols are also layered. The ISO model specifies the following layers, as diagrammed in Figure 37.

Physical layer   As with the "postal protocols" discussed above, the lowest layer of the ISO model concerns the physical process of getting the data from one point to another. As with the postal case, there can be several choices for the transmission method, many of which have been discussed in Chapter 2.

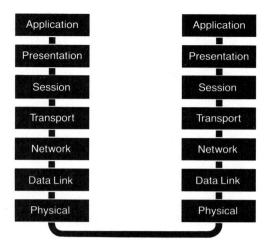

Figure 37. ISO layered model for protocols

Data link layer   During the process of getting from one point to another, data bits may be subject to errors. Also, it may be desirable to send bits for a variety of purposes, for example, some bits may be user data and others may be for control purposes. To ensure that transmission errors can be detected, and to permit user data bits and control bits to be sent over the same physical layer, data communication systems send bits in groups called "frames." The assembly and transmission of frames is accomplished by the data link layer.

The data link layer may also perform additional tasks, but these depend on the network environment. Since the ISO model was developed for protocols used over long error-prone common carrier channels of varying transmission speeds, a true implementation of the ISO model provides error control and flow control at several layers, including the data link layer. Local area networks, however, can often assume a relatively error-free transmission medium of constant speed. Depending upon the validity of those assumptions, error control and flow control features at lower levels of the model can be eliminated, saving substantial hardware and software overhead. These features are retained at higher levels, but are used infrequently enough (if the foregoing assumptions are valid) so that the high cost of performing them there is rarely felt.

If, however, one wants to have error control in the data link layer, it can be accomplished as part of the process of dividing the data up into frames. The frames are analogous to the letters delivered by the post office, in that they have a "greeting" (called a "header") and a closing (called a "frame check sequence"). The headers contain message numbering that indicates the number of the message being transmitted and the number of the last good message received (or in some cases the number of the next message expected). The frame check sequences are (usually) 16- or 32-bit quantities that are the result of specific mathematical operations performed on the bits that constitute the message. If the frame check sequence contained in the message agrees with the frame check sequence generated by the receiving station on the basis of the received data, the receiving station sends a positive acknowledgment to the transmitting station, either immediately or as part of a subsequent transmitted message header. If the frame check sequence does not agree, a negative acknowledgment (or in some cases no acknowledgment) is sent. The transmitting station responds to this situation, possibly after a time-out period, by retransmitting the message.

As indicated above, an additional task that could be performed in the data link layer is flow control for the transmission system, which could be useful in networks with transmission links of varying speeds. (Transmission flow control can also be accomplished by higher-level software.) In networks where the host computers are also of varying speed, it is also necessary to have flow control between the hosts, but that is provided in a higher layer rather than in the data link layer.

The physical layer and the data link layer are typically implemented in hardware, but the functions of the layers above these are usually implemented in firmware or software.

Network, transport, session, and presentation layers

Network, transport, session, and presentation layers each provide a service for the layers above them, and the functions delegated to each layer vary somewhat in different protocols. Among the services provided are the following.

1. *Route selection*

    A "global" address for the destination may be added, i.e., an address which will specify the destination no matter which combination of transmission links is used.

2. *Congestion control for the links*

    The number of messages queued up for transmission over various links may be limited.

3. *Creation of an error-free sequenced stream*

    Many network services require a reliable, sequenced, error-free stream of data between the two ends of the connection (a "virtual circuit"). Other services can make use of more primitive facilities. For example, in some cases ("datagrams") it may be acceptable to have data delivered with only a certain probability of success, and applications may make use of data that are delivered out of order. If a reliable, sequenced, error-free stream is needed, it is provided the middle layer protocols, usually those in the transport layer.

4. *Multiplexing*

It is possible to utilize multiple network connections for high throughput, or to multiplex several transport connections onto the same network connection for economy. Either case must be transparent to the next higher layer.

5. *Congestion control for the hosts*

As indicated in conjunction with the data link discussion, additional flow control functionality, primarily associated with keeping fast hosts from overrunning slow hosts, can exist at a higher level of the protocol.

6. *User interface*

One of the higher levels of the protocol, usually the session layer, is the user's interface to the network and contains the software necessary for a user to establish a connection with another host. The user can then log on and become an interactive user on that machine, or the user can access that machine simply to transfer a file. There should be security mechanisms to protect against unauthorized access to the services or files on the network, and there should be mechanisms for graceful recovery from broken connections.

7. *Message format interpretation*

One of the higher layers may define the meaning of bytes in the messages that are delivered by the lower layers. For example, the presentation layer might contain a program for interpreting messages destined for a file service program at the application layer. The interpretation program would tell the file service program, "The first bytes of the message contain a file name, followed by a carriage return and line feed. The next bytes contain the user name of the file owner, followed by a carriage return and line feed. After that comes the file itself, followed by an end-of-file delimiter."

Application layer

The application layer contains the programs which perform the tasks desired by the users. Examples include the various service programs discussed in Chapters 1 and 9; file service programs, printer service programs, and mail service programs are all examples of application layer programs.

Alterations to the ISO model

As indicated in the discussion of the data link layer, many protocols, especially those written for use on local area networks, follow the ISO model only very loosely. In addition to the deletion of features from various layers, some layers, such as the session layer, may not be implemented at all. Furthermore, some protocols optimize performance by providing direct communications between higher and lower layers (skipping intervening layers) when passing information that is frequently required by the higher layer.

References

Davies, D. W., et al. *Computer Networks and Their Protocols.* New York: John Wiley & Sons, 1979.

Information Processing Systems—Open Systems Interconnection—Basic Reference Model. Draft International Standard ISO/DIS 7498, 1982.

McNamara, John E. *Technical Aspects of Data Communication*, 2nd ed. Bedford, Mass.: Digital Press, 1982.

Tanenbaum, Andrew S. *Computer Networks.* Englewood Cliffs, N.J.: Prentice Hall, 1981.

9   Servers[*]

As discussed in previous chapters, local area networks are a method of allowing the users of personal computers to have shared access to data and resources such as storage, input/output, and communications devices. In this chapter, the concept of shared access to resources will be discussed in greater detail. Both the advantages of shared access and some of the outstanding problems will be explored.

Economies of scale

The past twenty years have seen a rapid decline in the cost of electronic devices thanks to advances in the design and fabrication of integrated circuits. The most dramatic cost declines have taken place in memories, as these circuits are highly regular (repetitive) and can be easily designed and fabricated. Furthermore, memories are useful in all computer systems and thus enjoy the high production volumes that drive down unit costs. Microprocessor costs have also been brought down by the combination of regular design and high-volume production, but these factors are less strong in microprocessors than in memories, so the cost reductions have been less dramatic.

The declining costs of microprocessors and memories have extended into other electronic devices where microprocessors and memories either were already in use or were introduced to cut costs. For example, microprocessor-assisted data recovery techniques have brought improvements in disk cost and performance by allowing increased disk speeds and bit densities without loss of data. Microelectronics has also come to the aid of printer designers to enable them to produce better copies more cheaply.

The role of microelectronics in assisting disk and printer designers has been very important, as both of these devices are basically mechanical, and while advances have been made in mechanical systems, cost declines like those in the microelectronics area have not occurred. The microelectronic enhancements have allowed disks and

*This chapter was coauthored with Larry W. Allen.

printers to amortize the high cost of their mechanical parts over more bits stored, or over more and better copies produced. The cost per bit stored or the cost per page produced thus declines dramatically as larger disks and faster printers are used. This is essentially an economy-of-scale effect, and is one of the most important reasons that these devices should be shared.

Communications channels also have economies of scale, but for a different reason. Here, the primary reason is historical. Telephone networks have always been organized in terms of the "voice grade line," a channel of slightly less than 4 kiloHertz bandwidth used to transmit a voice conversation. Larger amounts of bandwidth have been available in specified sizes—the Group (12 voice channels), the Super Group (60 voice channels), and so forth. Modern public data networks offer services in terms of bits per second rather than kiloHertz of bandwidth, but sizing—2400 bps, 4800 bps, 9600 bps, 56,000 bps, and so on—still exists. Note in particular the large jump between 9600 and 56,000 bps; it is such jumps in facility sizes that make the sharing of communications channels so attractive.

Controlled sharing of data

The benefits of local area networks include not only economies of scale but also shared access to a common data base. Shared access to a common data base is not a new concept; it has been offered by timesharing systems for many years. A major design goal of the timesharing systems of the mid-1960s, especially those used in research environments, was the ability to provide controlled sharing of information between users. When there are many people working on a project, it is very important that they be able to have shared access to the data and programs that they are developing. At the same time, users have to be able to control the access to the data and programs against other people who might not have the privilege to see them or change them. With the evolution toward personal computers, a problem has arisen that people can no longer conveniently share data and programs, especially those stored in personal computers that have local disks. For example, if a new version of the operating system comes out, but it does not get copied to everyone's disk, chaos can result. In contrast, shared access to a common file system would allow controlled access to the latest data and software.

The phrase "controlled sharing" is very important, however, as some people buy personal computers to do spreadsheet analysis and things they consider to be security risks, such as employee salary planning and corporate financial forecasts. They would rather not do these things on a timesharing system because they don't trust the people running the timesharing system. Thus, one of the issues that has to be solved in the design of personal computer networks is the provision of security equal to or better than that of timesharing systems. Even then, some users will want their machines to be capable of running some applications without a network connection. The security issue is discussed in somewhat greater detail in the "Problems" section later in this chapter.

Achieving resource sharing via servers

Having established that economies of scale dictate that access to certain mechanical devices should be shared, and that operational requirements often require that access to data should be shared, the question arises, How can such shared access be accomplished? The sharing of resources and data in a local area network is accomplished by means of hardware/software packages called "servers." While diagrams of local area networks have created an impression that servers are dedicated computers which each provide a single service, such as a "file server" or a "printer server," this is not necessarily the case. Such dedicated computers do exist and are being sold by various vendors as solutions to specific problems, but it is better to think of servers as *programs* that provide services, rather than as specific pieces of hardware. Thinking of servers as software will be increasingly appropriate in the future, as the evolution of networks is causing new servers to be developed, many of which are packages of software that run on almost any computer.

To further understand the concept of servers, it is useful to examine some specific examples, starting with a common type of server, the print server.

The print server

A print server is a hardware/software package which allows anyone on the network to have access to a printing service. The hardware includes an ordinary line printer or a high-resolution laser printer. The software receives and buffers a file of information, which may come from a personal computer with its own disk or may come from a shared file system (file server) from which it was delivered at the request of a personal computer user. The file is usually transferred to the printer server in a format which can be understood by the printer. In the case of a line printer, this would be ASCII and would include page headers and other printer control information. Since the formatting has already been done, the software required in the print server is relatively simple and consists primarily of programs that queue multiple requests for printing service, although there may also be special typesetting and graphics software.

The file server

A file server is a program that provides user access to disks or other mass storage devices. In addition to storing and retrieving files as specified by the users, the program provides protection from unauthorized reading and writing, and similar features currently found in file service routines associated with the operating systems run on time-sharing systems. Thus, its principal function is to allow users to have controlled shared access to common data bases and programs.

The disk server

A disk server is a simplified version of the file server. Its primary function is to achieve economy of scale by dividing a large disk into the sections to which individual users have access. Controlled shared access to common data bases and programs is provided in very limited form, if at all.

Backup service

In a network providing network-wide file access by means of a file server, a backup service could back up the information on the file server onto magnetic tape as periodically requested by the file service program. In addition, it could provide backup service for the personal computers' local disks (typically Winchester disks) on demand of the users or on demand of an operating system running in the personal computers.

Replicated data base service

Replicated data base service is similar to backup service but provides instant access to the backup copy by continuously maintaining a duplicate data base. This service is useful for applications, such as airline reservations, in which users need to get at their data at all times.

Mail service

One of the popular services provided by timesharing systems is the ability of one user to send mail to another. Memos, reminders, and inquiries about dinner plans are often exchanged in this way. Many networks provide a mail service in which one user may send mail to another user by addressing that user's personal computer via some sort of network address. In crude mail systems, if the destination is not available, the mail transmission fails. Good network mail services collect mail for network users and disperse it upon direct request by the user, or upon a request from the operating system in the user's computer. There are a number of reasons such a service is attractive:

1. A user could work from more than one personal computer.
2. A user's machine would not have to be operational to receive mail.
3. A user could have a portable terminal anywhere and dial into the network to receive mail.

In summary, a mail service would be exactly analogous to a post office box with remote access.

Remote compilation service

Compilers are large complicated programs that require a great deal of storage space and a great deal of time to run. The storage space requirements are not as serious a problem as the time requirements. Since compilation is part of the debugging loop, slow compilation wastes a valuable resource—a programmer's time. It is thus desirable to have as fast a compiler as possible, but the microprocessors found in personal computers may not be capable of the desired results. The use of a few moments' time on a large processor might be a better solution. This could be accomplished by having the large processor connected to the network and capable of running a program that supplied remote compilation service for the personal computer users.

Other computation-intensive services

In addition to compilation, programs such as circuit simulators, which predict the behavior of electrical circuits, require great amounts of storage space and run time. The complexity of modern hardware design has made such simulators a vital design aid, especially in areas where mistakes are extremely costly, such as VLSI design. Timesharing systems provide ready access to such programs, and they run in reasonable periods of time. Personal computers, on the other hand, have limited memory and speed, which slows the execution of these programs. In addition, many of these programs contain the characteristics of "corporate standard" parts, and updates occur constantly. If these programs could be accessed over the network as services available to all network users, considerable programmer time could be saved, and currency of the data could be assured.

Directory service

Directory or naming services are useful for performing a function analogous to the telephone directory. Users of large networks need to find where people are, and services need to be written to provide that capability. The service is basically a distributed data base system. Ideally, the service should be integrated into the system command language, making access to network objects and services nearly transparent.

Accounting service

This is an example of a service which provides a service for other service providers. If an organization wishes to charge users for their access to the network and for access to its associated services, an accounting service would be useful.

Communication service

Shared access to communication service may be desired for several reasons. In some cases, the communication service provides a physical extension of the local area network. Such an extension may be accomplished by means of relatively simple devices called "repeaters," "bridges," or "routers." These devices, and other methods of extending local area networks, are discussed in Chapter 10.

There are also cases in which access is desired to a variety of communications services available on other types of network. The most basic service is the capability of an organization to have two local area networks at distant sites and to use a public network to transport packets from one local area network to the other. A device at one local area network packages the data packets into a format appropriate to the long-haul network, which carries them across to a similar device at the other network. There the data packets are "unwrapped" and delivered to the other local area network.

Although the simple service described above is a very valuable service for lots of users, there are other services that need to be provided. One possible service is the capability for a user on a host, or user on a personal computer on a local area network, to be able to access a computer which is directly attached to one of the long-distance networks. A travel reservation system or data base service are possible examples. Such systems have traditionally only provided remote terminal access, but that type of access may involve protocols that are incompatible with those used on local area networks. Thus, a translating device would be required to provide this service by converting whatever terminal access protocol was being used in the local area network into a protocol used for host access in the long-distance network.

The devices which allow a local area network to connect to other types of network are moderately complex servers called "gateways." Gateways receive messages from one network, buffer them, and retransmit them onto another network. Since the physical media, access methods, message framing, error control, addressing, flow control, information formatting, and other characteristics of the two networks will usually be different, the gateway must deal with a complete set of protocol families for each network (i.e., all seven layers of the ISO model). A block diagram of a gateway's functions is shown in Figure 38.

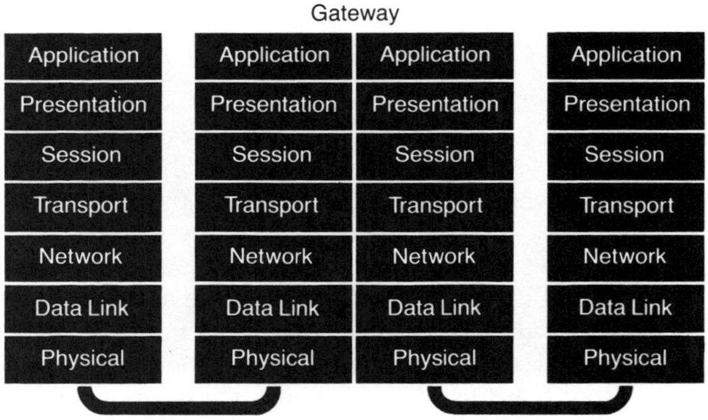

Gateway

Application	Application	Application	Application
Presentation	Presentation	Presentation	Presentation
Session	Session	Session	Session
Transport	Transport	Transport	Transport
Network	Network	Network	Network
Data Link	Data Link	Data Link	Data Link
Physical	Physical	Physical	Physical

Figure 38. Block diagram of a gateway's functions

Although gateways have been discussed as servers that connect between different types of network, they can also be used to provide translation among protocol families within a single network. For example, if the servers on the network use different protocol families, a gateway could be employed to provide users with access to all of the functions which the users might want, such as the ability to log into remote computers, transfer files between computers, and send mail to other users.

Terminal concentrators

While interest in local area networks has been primarily motivated by the problem of interconnecting personal computers and providing a method for them to have shared access to resources, many people will continue to use conventional terminals that contain little or no computational capability.

One model for connecting terminals to computers in a local area network is shown in Figure 39, wherein each terminal is directly attached to a computer. The arrangement shown is a logical outgrowth

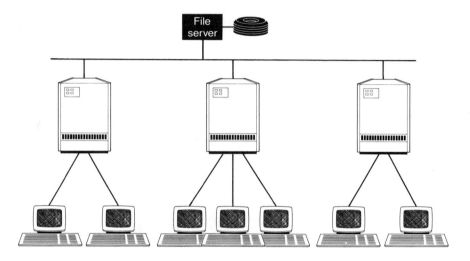

Figure 39. Terminals connected to hosts

of the timesharing system model of computing. In timesharing systems, the capabilities of the host computer were shared among terminal users who were directly connected to the host. The addition of a local area network allows the host to provide some of the services required by the personal computers on the network, but the users of conventional terminals still interact with the host in the traditional fashion. This method of connecting terminals is completely adequate and satisfactory until terminal users desire the capability of "remote log-in," that is, the ability to function as if they were logged in to a host other than the one to which they are directly wired. Such a situation might arise, if, for example, some other host had a particular program (such as a circuit simulator) that users wanted to run.

A "remote log-in" capability can certainly be implemented in a configuration such as that shown in Figure 39, but the relaying of terminal transactions through one host to another places computational overhead on both hosts. Furthermore, in systems where the computer into which a user is logged in provides the echo, the relaying action of intervening computer(s) may make the echoing process annoyingly slow.

The configuration shown in Figure 40 permits terminal users to connect to various host computers by connecting terminals not to hosts, but rather to "terminal concentrators." A terminal concentrator

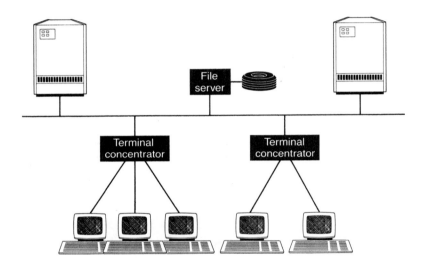

Figure 40. Terminals connected to concentrators

is typically a small, simple computer and a network interface. The echoing of typed characters can be performed by the terminal concentrator, providing users with response similar to that obtained by being directly connected to the host. The computational overhead associated with terminal communications occurs primarily in the concentrator, although the overhead of the network software operating in the host to support the concentrator is nonneglible.

Some of the software considerations for terminal concentrators are discussed in greater detail in Chapter 11.

Connecting to servers

To provide network services listed above to personal computer users in an automatic and transparent fashion, there is a need for an operating system running in the personal computers to be able to find hosts on the network that will supply the desired service. One example would be the access to a desired file among multiple file servers on the network.

If more than one server provides the desired service, criteria for selecting the server that will get the job need to be established. A possible selection criteria might be price, in which case servers would offer their services, and users who needed services would request bids. The servers would then bid, depending upon how busy they are, what kind of performance they could offer, and so on. The user would use the server offering the best bid, and the accounting could take place automatically. Price might be a less important factor in some kinds of service; for example, for printer servers, likely selection criteria would include copy quality, paper size, and physical proximity to the user.

Migration from timesharing to networks

Many of the services which have been described above are services which are currently provided to users by timesharing systems. It is neither necessary nor likely that conversion from the use of timesharing systems to the use of personal computers will take place overnight. A vast amount of time and money has been invested in timesharing systems and their associated software. It will take yet more time and money to translate that software over into personal computers. In the meantime, an evolutionary strategy will probably be pursued by most organizations.

The first step in the evolution toward personal computer use may be the connection of personal computers to existing timesharing systems via local area networks. In this way, existing software can be used to provide file services, printer services, and other services to the users of personal computers via the network in a fashion similar to, but not identical with, the way in which these services were formerly provided to terminal users via direct connections.

An example of a service that large systems could provide to personal computer users would be complex text formatting. The personal computer users on the network would be able to type in their files using the editor supplied on their personal computer, and then run the files through the text formatter on the large system to produce output. This would be implemented by writing a service program which was a remote utility on the timesharing system, that is, a program which permitted remote users to submit files to the existing text formatter program and receive formatted text.

Offering such services to users of the network, the timesharing systems would become service providers or servers.

Problems

In the previous section, we suggested that the services provided by local area network servers are a simple extension of the services previously provided by timesharing systems. To a large degree this is true, but the problems associated with providing services in a network environment are a lot more complex than those encountered in a timesharing system. Some especially difficult problems exist in the area of network management, software compatibility, and security.

Network management

Since the hardware in which service programs run may be unattended, the hardware and software need to be robust and recover from errors. As in timesharing systems, there should be service programs that keep logs of what tasks have been done and what errors have occurred. These logs are for maintenance and debugging purposes, so only information from the most recent day or two needs to be stored.

Since the hardware in which the service programs run may not be equipped with console terminals or bulk loading devices, the hardware and software need to have network management functions such as the capability of being downline loaded. There also needs to be a capability of sending messages over the network to change the parameters in the server when certain service actions are performed, such as the changing of paper types in print servers. Finally, status and error conditions need to be remotely readable.

Software compatibility

In organizations that had a single timesharing system, software compatibility between the programs that provided services and the user programs was not a problem. The operating system, usually provided by the computer manufacturer, made sure that users had convenient and compatible access to the services they needed.

When organizations decentralized their data processing, groups within the organization often chose widely differing computer systems to meet their needs. As long as each system was freestanding and independent of all other systems, no problems arose. As was indicated at the beginning of this chapter, however, technological advances have now made it attractive to have computer "partial systems" (a processor and memory) on each desk while sharing access to resources where economies of scale exist or sharing access where operational considerations merit such sharing. Software compatibility between the programs that provide the shared services and the user programs is now a problem. In addition, there may be incompatibilities between the protocol families associated with the services and those associated with the users.

Security

Security in local area networks is a major problem. While the problem extends to all of the network services, it is most apparent in the operation of file servers.

Users of file servers want to guarantee that their files cannot be read, modified, or deleted without their permission. Specifying who has permission to access a file in what manner is usually done in a timesharing operating system by means of an access control list, which is essentially a list of people or groups of people who are authorized to read, modify, or delete the file. In a conventional operating system, this provides a good level of security, as the operating system has fairly powerful means available for identifying users. It is very hard for a user to forge an identification because passwords are encrypted and kept secret, and the operating system's data structures are protected so that the normal user can't read them.

In a network environment, a number of problems arise in utilizing access control lists. Every user has to have a network-wide identification so that when a user requests access to a file on the file server, the file server can tell unambiguously who the user is and perform a comparison against the access list to see if that user has permission to access the file in the fashion being requested. Achieving user identification in a secure fashion is not as simple as in the single-system case, however. Local area networks are demonstrably not secure, especially broadcast networks in which everyone can see every packet going by. Once a malicious user has seen a packet go by with someone's identification, that user can record it and play it back later, forge a copy of a packet with the other user's identification, or do any of a number of things to subvert the system. Thus, there is a dual need in the network. First, there is a need for a network-wide method of user identification so that users logging in get recognized by all the file servers. Second, there is a need for a user to be able to present his or her identification to the file servers in such a way that the file server can be sure of the user's identity.

There are some ways that encryption can be used to meet these needs. For example, a scheme has been proposed in which the user and the server securely obtain a key which they can use to communicate with each other. An encrypted data stream is produced such that no one can listen in, and the user and server are authenticated to each other at the same time.

For file storage, other types of protection are necessary. One approach is to actually encrypt the data in the file. Simply encrypting the data might not protect the file from damage or deletion, however. Furthermore, the encryption technique used would have to be quite robust, as persons attempting unauthorized access to a file would typically have a substantial amount of time and computational resources available to use in mounting their attack.

In addition to these problems with encrypted files, there may be problems with backup, and there is certainly a problem with lost keys. If the key is lost in a simple transaction, that's not a serious problem, as the two ends can start over again. If a key is lost on a file containing important data, the user is "up the creek without a paddle."

Over the next few years we can anticipate a number of developments in the security area, with a variety of techniques being used depending upon the level of protection desired. Security of all types imposes a time and expense overhead, and everyone who wants security must pick a method which involves the best tradeoff of expense and protection level.

10 Extending local area networks

The search for the perfect network

People considering the purchase of a local area network often search for a single network design that will solve all of their problems. Network manufacturers engage in a similar search for a single product offering that will cover the market. Neither group ever fully succeeds, as there are some important restrictions to their search.

Figure 41 shows the relationship between the bandwidth of local area network media and the cost of the network. In this figure, the cost of the media (and installation) is shown increasing modestly with bandwidth. The reason for this is that installation costs generally dominate, making it relatively unimportant whether one installs twisted pair or fiber optics. It is this part of local area network cost that generates the statement that "in local area networks, bandwidth is cheap." The media cost is not the whole story, however.

The expense of driving the medium generally increases at a more rapid rate than the installed cost of the medium. The line drivers, modems, transceivers, and so on, for high-bandwidth media generally require more expensive components than for low-bandwidth media. Furthermore, many high-bandwidth media, such as broadband, are multiplexed in some fashion, thus requiring modems or transceivers that are more complex than the devices used to drive low-bandwidth nonmultipexed media.

The control logic to drive high-bandwidth media is usually more expensive than that required to drive low-bandwidth media. Not only are high-speed logic families such as ECL more expensive than conventional logic such as TTL, but also the architecture of high-speed controllers generally involves more processors and more parallel data paths than that of low-speed controllers.

Finally, the interfaces associated with high-bandwidth media must buffer data transmitted to and received from the media to prevent data rates to or from the associated network station that are beyond the station's capabilities. The higher the bandwidth of the media, the more buffer memory is required. Despite the allegation that memory is very cheap, $2n$ bytes of memory is always more expensive than n bytes of memory (assuming the same size and technology of memory chips in both cases).

Note that the axes of the graph have been intentionally left uncalibrated because dollar costs for given amounts of bandwidth change every year. The important point is that more bandwidth costs more money; hence, a local area network which has exactly the right amount of bandwidth for the user's needs (including future growth, traffic peaks, and desired delay characteristics) will cost less than a network that has several times the amount of bandwidth required.

Despite the additional cost of excess bandwidth, some excess may permit other economies, such as the use of diskless workstations. In addition, an excess would allow for unanticipated network growth.

Figure 42 shows the relationship between the throughput of a local area network and the distance spanned by the network. This figure

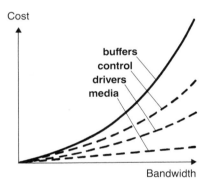

Figure 41. Bandwidth
versus cost

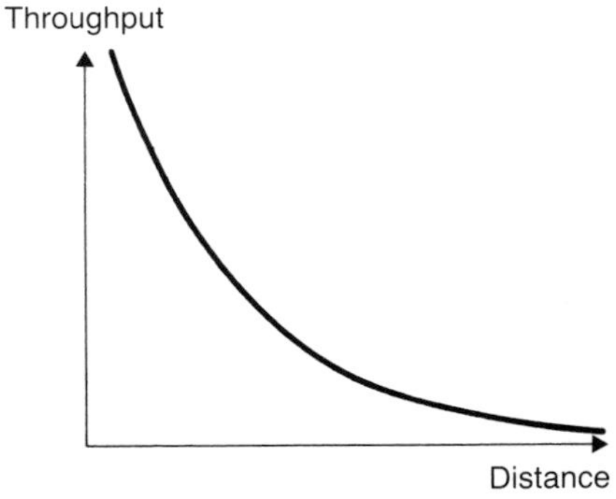

Figure 42. Distance versus
throughput

does not have calibrated axes because throughput versus distance characteristics vary widely with the access arbitration method used. For example, a CSMA/CD network will require longer minimum packet sizes when the distance increases so that all collisions can be detected. The longer minimum packet sizes decrease the effective throughput. A token passing network, either bus or ring, will experience greater delays in larger networks, especially as the number of stations increases, since each station contains buffers through which all traffic must pass.

The above figures and associated discussions seem to imply that bandwidth and throughput are evil, as they increase costs and decrease distances. Anyone who has ever used a graphics workstation, or anyone who has "stepped up" from a 300-bps terminal to a 9600-bps terminal, will dispute that idea, declaring that the human mind is the most valuable resource there is and should not be wasted waiting for a screen to fill. As with most things, the best solutions in local area networking often lie in between the extremes of ultimate low cost and ultimate high performance.

To achieve a compromise approach to installing the optimum local area network, two approaches can be considered:

1. Install high-speed, short-distance networks and interconnect them.
2. Install high-speed, short-distance networks and lower-speed, long-distance networks and interconnect them.

In both cases, there may be limitations on network performance through the interconnection points.

Interconnecting high-speed networks

In bus systems, the signal levels and waveforms on the bus degenerate with distance from the transmitting station. At some point, the signals require regeneration by means of a device which will receive the weakened signals, interpert their digital values, and transmit new signals onto the next segment of the bus. To maintain the bus architecture, the regeneration device must be capable of performing this function for signals arriving from either side of the device, that is, from either bus segment to which it is attached.

In ring systems, the signal levels and waveforms on the bus also degenerate with distance from the transmitting station, but the next station on the ring performs the signal regeneration function without need for a specific device.

In local area networks requiring signal regeneration by a specific device, this is accomplished by a device called a "repeater."

Repeaters

While some refer to this device as a repeater, ISO documents call it a "physical relay" or "level 1 relay." The function of the device can best be understood by looking at Figure 43.

The repeater does not perform any of the data link functions such as addressing, error control, or flow control. Although it may do some timing correction and waveform regeneration, it has minimal effect on signal propagation delay, as there is no software involved and no layer-to-layer interfacing.

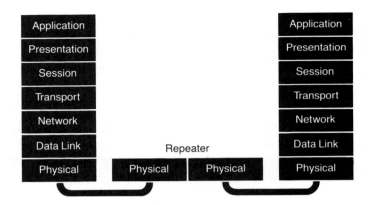

Figure 43. Protocol relayed by a repeater

The repeater is, however, limited to connecting two identical physical links. If the physical links differ in any way—media, topology, or access method—a more complex device will be required.

Bridges

When it is desirable to extend a local area network by employing a different type of physical link, a "bridge" may be useful. ISO documents refer to this device as a "data link relay" or "level 2 relay." The function of the device can best be understood by looking at Figure 44.

In contrast to the repeater, which acts upon the bits transferred between the physical layers of the two stations, a bridge acts upon the frames transferred between the data link layers of the two stations. Since the bridge must access each of the physical links according to the access rules of that particular network, and may not be able to achieve instant access, the bridge must be capable of storing and forwarding frames.

Since bridges store-and-forward frames, they can examine the address fields in the frames and forward messages based on knowledge of which network contains the destination node. The ability of a bridge to perform this traffic filtering function depends upon the sophistication of the bridge's algorithms for determining the location of various nodes, and depends upon the similarity of the data link protocols used by the nodes that are communicating via the bridge.

If the addressing algorithms and data link protocol similarities permit traffic filtering to work well, bridges can increase both the number of supported nodes and the area covered, since each of the networks connected can be configured within its own design and performance limitations.

A bridge offers much more functionality than a repeater and is particularly attractive for its ability to interconnect different types of local area network. Since it does more handling of the information passing through, it introduces more delay than a repeater.

Routers

A router is also referred to as an "intermediate system," "network relay," or "level 3 relay." Its relationship to the ISO model is shown in Figure 45.

Routers differ from bridges in two ways. First, in contrast to the bridge, which acts upon the frames transferred between the data link layers of the two stations, a router acts upon the packets transferred between the network layers of the two stations. Second, bridges and

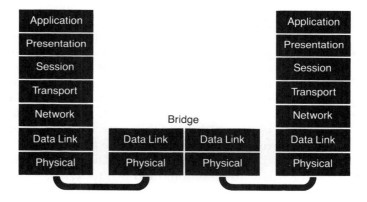

Figure 44. Protocols relayed by a bridge

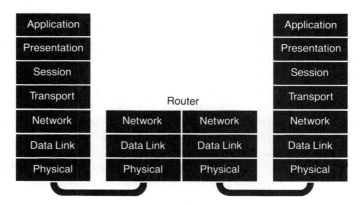

Figure 45. Protocols relayed by a router

repeaters are (ideally) invisible to the end stations communicating through them, but routers are known to the end stations, and the end stations explicitly address them when routing service is desired.

An example of a node asking for the services of a router occurs in some networks when some (or all) of the network nodes do not know the state of the network. If such a node has a message it wants to send, it sends the message data packets to a router. The router has a record of network status because various nodes have periodically sent messages to it confirming their existence and announcing their network addresses. The router maintains this information in a table, and can thus determine whether the destination address is on that network or elsewhere. If the address is on the network, the router simply retransmits the message. If the address is not on the network, the router forwards the message to the appropriate other network directly or via a gateway.

In other networks, the addressing is arranged so that the transmitting station can look at the destination address and determine whether the destination host is attached to the same network. If it is, the station simply transmits; if not, the transmitting station sends a message to a router or gateway which will forward it.

It is also possible for each node on the network to maintain its own routing tables, but this consumes CPU time both in performing the routing and in updating the tables.

A router offers more functionality than a bridge, primarily in being able to do routing, and by providing some management of how much traffic is carried over various communications links to other networks (rather than mere filtering). Since it does more handling of the information passing through, it introduces more delay than a bridge.

Gateways

So far, each of the communications devices discussed—repeater, bridge, router—has been shown in a diagram where the device has little if any effect upon the protocol layers above it. If the two communicating stations have identical transport level, session level, presentation level, and application level protocols, the transparency of the devices discussed is desirable. However, there are many different local area networks in use, and many different protocol families. To connect two networks that use different protocol families, or to support two protocol families on the same physical network, a complete translation between the protocol families is required, and the devices discussed so far are not adequate.

Complete translation between protocol families is accomplished by devices called "gateways," "interworking units," or "level 7 relays." Such a device is shown in Figure 46.

As can be deduced from the figure, a gateway can connect any network to any other network and provides the full range of functionality from bit handling at the physical level up through framing, error detection, routing, flow control, message byte field interpretation, and so on. In return for all this functionality and flexibility, the propagation delay for a message to traverse a gateway is orders of magnitude beyond that to traverse a simple repeater. However, if the gateway is being used to access a service that cannot be provided by the local area network, it is a price that must be paid.

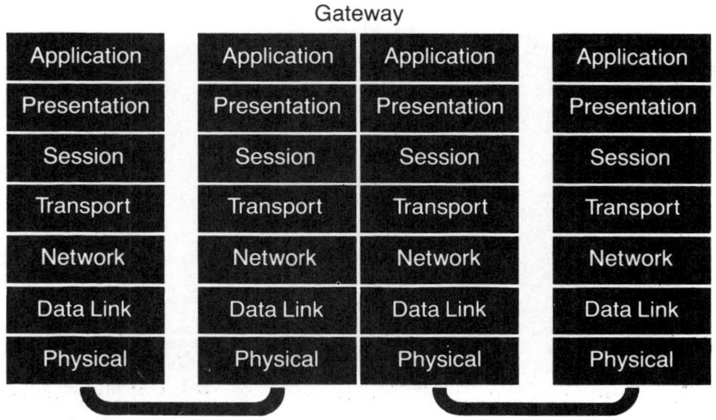

Gateway

Application	Application	Application	Application
Presentation	Presentation	Presentation	Presentation
Session	Session	Session	Session
Transport	Transport	Transport	Transport
Network	Network	Network	Network
Data Link	Data Link	Data Link	Data Link
Physical	Physical	Physical	Physical

Figure 46. Protocols relayed by a gateway

Interconnecting different types of network

The previous paragraphs described the use of gateways to interconnect differing protocol families on the same network or to interconnect different networks. The possibility that different networks could be interconnected suggests that one could create a local area network that utilized a combination of network topologies, access methods, and media to achieve a maximally cost-effective network. The remainder of this chapter will discuss some hybrid networks created by interconnecting different types of local area network.

A hybrid network should ideally provide high performance for those users who need it, low-cost connections for those with more modest requirements, and a migration path to provide higher performance for more people as that performance becomes more economical.

The systems shown below are only starting points. They are not intended as recommendations, but rather as objects of discussion. Hopefully, anyone who has read this book, its references, and other texts available can think of many other interesting configurations.

Ethernet and PBX   The advantages of this arrangement (Figure 47) are that terminals
which require very high bandwidth, such as graphics stations and
diskless personal computers, get it via direct connection to Ethernet;
stations (terminals and disk-equipped personal computers) which require lower bandwidth (64 Kbps) get it via the PBX. Assuming there are
a small number of high-speed stations, the large cables and distance
limitations of Ethernet will not be a problem. Assuming there are a
great many slow-speed stations, the convenience of PBX wiring will be
attractive. On the other hand, the PBX does not need to be designed to
handle the very high bandwidth required by the graphics stations. Finally, the number of low-speed and high-speed stations can be altered
fairly painlessly.

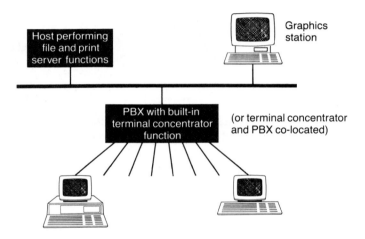

Figure 47. Ethernet and PBX

Wire-center token   The advantages of this system (Figure 48) are basically the same as
ring and PBX   those of the Ethernet with PBX system, except the advantages and disadvantages of wire-center token rings are substituted for the advantages and disadvantages of Ethernet.

Ethernet   The advantages of this arrangement (Figure 49) are that terminals
and terminal   which require very high bandwidth, such as graphics stations and
concentrators with   diskless personal computers, get it via direct connection to the Ether-
long line drivers   net; slow-speed stations which require lower bandwidth (64 Kbps) get
it via RS-422 or RS-423 lines to terminal concentrators in telephone
equipment closets. Assuming there are few high-speed stations, the

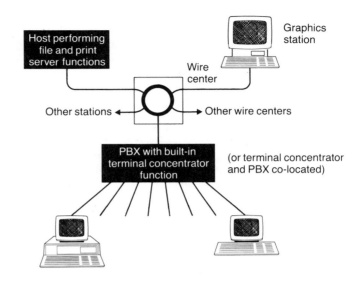

Figure 48. Wire-center token ring and PBX

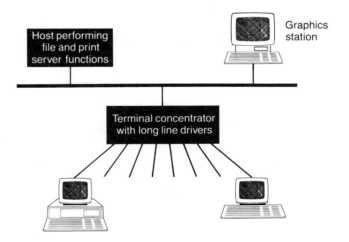

*Figure 49. Ethernet terminal concentrators
with long line drivers*

limitations of Ethernet will not be a problem. Assuming there are many slow-speed stations, the convenience of RS-422/RS-423 wiring will be attractive. As with the previous systems, the number of low-speed and high-speed stations can be altered fairly painlessly.

Wire-center token ring and terminal concentrators with long line drivers

The advantages of this system (Figure 50) are basically the same as those of the Ethernet with terminal concentrators with long line drivers, except the advantages and disadvantages of wire-center token rings are substituted for the advantages and disadvantages of Ethernet.

Ethernet, wire-center token ring, PBX system

The advantages of this arrangement (Figure 51) are that terminals which require very high bandwidth, such as graphics stations, get it via connection to the Ethernet or connection to a token ring, depending on the vendor of the station equipment. The wide acceptance and simplicity of Ethernet connections are an advantage here. In addition, the high traffic capabilities, convenient conversion to fiber optics, and distance capabilities of the token ring are capitalized upon to form the "spine" network. Stations (terminals and personal computers) which require lower bandwidth (64 Kbps) get it via the PBX, where the low cost of connection, convenient wiring, and opportunity to integrate with voice-related office automation functions are attractive features.

Ethernet, wire-center token ring, Ethernet system

The advantages of this arrangement (Figure 52) are that terminals which require very high bandwidth, such as graphics stations and diskless personal computers, get it via connection to the Ethernet, where the wide acceptance and simplicity of Ethernet connections are an advantage. The advantages of the token ring are capitalized upon to form the spine network. Stations (terminals and disk-equipped personal computers) which require lower bandwidth (64 Kbps) get it via Ethernet terminal concentrators, possibly equipped with long line drivers to utilize convenient wiring.

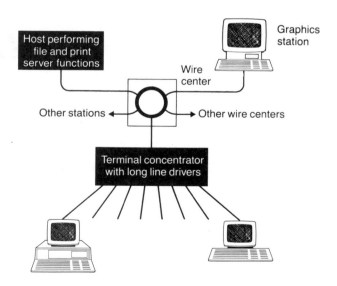

Figure 50. Wire-center-token-ring terminal concentrators with long line drivers

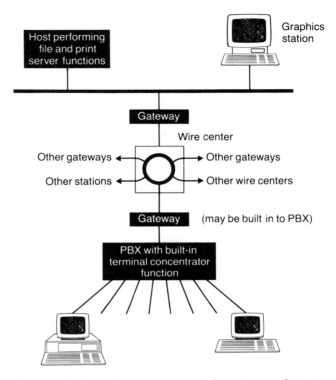

Figure 51. Ethernet, wire-center token ring, and PBX

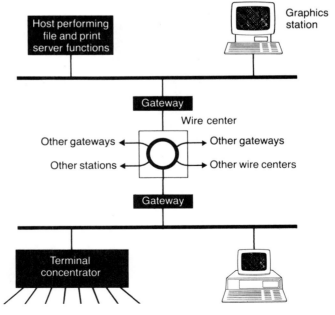

Figure 52. Ethernet, wire-center token ring, and Ethernet

Disadvantages

Before leaving the subject of hybrid networks, one must mention that there are some disadvantages to the network arrangements shown in the preceding figures. These include the following.

1. *Dealing with multiple vendors*

   Dealing with multiple vendors can result in a great deal of frustration when something breaks, as each vendor will be unsure whether it is his equipment that is causing the problem and will tend to blame the other vendors. Furthermore, maintenance becomes more complex, as each vendor uses different design and documentation practices. Finally, volume purchase discounts will be less when the business is spread among multiple vendors.

2. *Software incompatibilities*

   A diverse collection of local area network types need not mean a diverse collection of software, but it certainly increases the likelihood of this.

The problems associated with administering large networks, especially those made up of differing types of local area network, are discussed in greater detail in the next chapter.

Summary

Local area networks are a way of providing shared access to resources in a fashion which makes maximally efficient use of the technological trends of this decade. There are a number of topologies, access methods, media, hardware designs, and software designs being developed to achieve the full promise of local area networks, but none of them are panaceas. The plurality of solutions available is good for the student, the designer, and the customer, because the lack of a single solution provides the student and the designer with incentive to find one, and provides the customer with the chance to buy a highly specialized network to best meet his or her needs. Unfortunately, the diversity of networks available means that standards are few (or too many, depending upon how you look at it), a particularly bothersome problem in the software area.

11 Administrative considerations for large networks[*]

There are a number of local area networks on the market which are small systems dedicated to a particular application or group of applications. For a small business, the installation of one or two of these systems will provide the benefits of local area network technology in a simple and straightforward fashion. However, for a large organization such as a multibuilding business complex or a university, the installation of dozens of local area networks can pose problems. The installation of a single local area network to span the entire property is also frequently infeasible. This chapter explores the problems associated with installing local area networks that serve large numbers of users, and suggests some solutions or at least some ways of thinking about solutions.

The need for centralized administration

Before the advent of local area networks, or even the advent of mini-computers, large businesses and universities did all of their computation in large computer centers. The traditional large computer facility consisted of a giant processor housed in an impressive room surrounded by smaller rooms containing the offices of the hardware and software experts who kept the great machine going, made modifications to its hardware and software, and resolved the users' questions and problems. Operation of such a facility was on a formal basis, because users of the facility expected reasonable service on a continuing basis, and this required serious and formal attention to the issues of maintenance, planning, and funding.

The advent of the minicomputer changed all this. A small computer

[*]This chapter is paraphrased from memoranda of Dr. David D. Clark of the M.I.T. Laboratory for Computer Science.

facility, such as a minicomputer shared by a few users, could be satis-factorily operated on an informal basis. Each user personally knew who was responsible for which pieces of hardware and software, and could walk down the hall to the appropriate person's office whenever a question or problem arose.

Local area networks that interconnect only a few small computers within the same "interest group" have had little effect upon this infor-mal way of doing business. However, large local area networks that span a college campus or multiple buildings of a large company have brought with them new administrative requirements:

1. The capital required to purchase the equipment for large local area networks is typically beyond the budget of a single user group.
2. Professional workmen, rather than volunteers, must install the ca-bles, and they must install them in conduit and duct space that is often in limited supply.
3. Planning for future expansion must be done in a fashion which en-sures adequate services for everyone, but without wasteful duplica-tion of effort.

The above requirements can be met with the best economies of scale if a central network is installed by a central group. In addition, the net-work should be administered and maintained by a central group, be-cause once the network has been installed, the network users will typ-ically expect the same reasonable service on a continuing basis that characterized the large timesharing systems. To achieve that level of service, attention must be paid to the same issues of maintenance, planning, and funding that were the keys to success for the large com-puter facility. These issues are more complex in the case of a network, however, because of the distributed nature of the hardware and soft-ware, and the high degree of independence exercised by the managers of the computer systems connected to the network.

Of the administrative issues to be considered, the installation and maintenance of hardware and software are among the most important, because both are continuing processes which will interact with the other administrative issues—that is, planning and funding. While some of the hardware installation issues have already been discussed in other parts of the book, hardware maintenance issues and software installation and maintenance issues deserve detailed treatment here.

Hardware maintenance responsibility

The most obvious hardware maintenance requirement is the identifica-tion of responsibility when a network component breaks. Thus, for each piece of equipment (including cables), there must be a clear defi-nition of maintenance responsibility. Since a complete network in-cludes both the centrally administered network facility and the individual host computers attached to the network, it is necessary to define a boundary of responsibility which surrounds the centrally administered network facility. Since the components which are within this boundary will vary, it may be easier to define the boundary by saying which devices are outside the boundary. Typically, host machines and locally run networks which connect clusters of machines will be outside the boundary.

Software installation and maintenance responsibility

Another important administrative requirement is that connecting to the central network must not create an excessive software implementation and maintenance effort for the host machines. This consideration is very important, as the implementation of network protocols is not trivial. Network protocols are a specialized type of software, and since networking is a recent trend in computing, the number of people who are familiar with protocol programming is limited. To implement a complete protocol package for a host machine can easily represent more than a man-year of effort, even if an experienced programmer can be found. Furthermore, the installation of a new protocol package represents a substantial modification to the operating system of the host, and this implies a commitment to the continued maintenance and upgrade of that software.

There are several ways to minimize the effort of software implementation. First, one could restrict the number of different machines and operating systems which are installed, and thus reduce the total number of software packages which must be maintained. Some organizations have shown a willingness to do this in certain areas of computer procurement, such as word processing equipment, but this may have been more driven by operator training considerations than by a desire to limit software proliferation. Second, one could assign the responsibility for locally implemented network software to service groups. Third, one can take advantage, wherever possible, of vendor-supplied software. Many manufacturers include a complete implementation of some network protocol family as part of their software packages. To the extent possible, use of this software is highly desirable because it avoids local modification of the vendor software entirely.

The next few pages will explore these alternatives in greater detail. Before choosing among alternatives, however, there should be a discussion of the goals for network software.

Goals for network software

The first goal should be to permit all of the machines which speak any particular family of protocols to communicate with each other. This goal is relatively simple, as it does not attempt to solve the problem of allowing machines speaking one family of protocols to talk to those which speak another. By analogy, this goal is the same as building a telephone system which permits French speakers to speak to other French speakers and English speakers to speak to other English speakers, but does not attempt to solve the problem of language translation.

The second goal should be to provide access to specific services which an organization wishes to offer to all users. Examples include the printer servers, backup servers, and mail servers discussed in Chapter 9. Another example is providing "remote log-in," by which all of the terminals scattered throughout the buildings of an organization can have uniform access to all of the host machines.

In addition to providing access to services provided by hosts on the network, the network should also provide access to services provided by external vendors. Examples include circuit-switched and packet-switched long haul networks, which in turn provide access to other external services such as data base marketing services, on-line newspapers, and on-line travel reservation systems.

It should be noted that unlike the first goal, this second goal raises the problem of incompatible protocols to some degree, for it is necessary to make services accessible even though the host requesting the service may speak a protocol that is different from the host providing the service.

The third and final goal is to provide communication between two machines which speak different protocols. This is the hardest goal, and is akin to providing language translation as part of telephone service. To provide arbitrary conversion between all protocol families in support of all applications in any large organization is not a reasonable requirement for a central network. However, for restricted applications, such as the transfer of mail between the various hosts, the central network should attempt to solve the problem.

Multiple protocol support

There are several ways in which the goal of universal communication among hosts on a network could be met. These include providing standard protocols at every level, providing separate logical links for each protocol, providing a standard network protocol, and using access networks and spine networks.

Method 1: standard protocols at every level

In the first alternative, one could provide a standard protocol definition at every level, and require that any two machines that wish to speak to each other, whatever their native protocol, translate their protocols into the standard protocol. This requirement would be analogous to passing a law that said that everybody in the country, no matter what his native language, must translate all of his speech into the "standard language of the land" in order to speak to anybody. Two Englishmen could not use English between themselves, but would have to go through the intermediate stage of translating communications into the required language. Aside from the obvious costs that everyone must learn the standard language and everyone must go through the translation phase, which is somewhat expensive, there is a subtle problem which arises; that is, the ability to express ideas is limited to those ideas which can be expressed in the standard language. If there is some nuance of expression which the standard language does not contain, then it has been denied to all speakers of all languages, even if their communication within their own language depended heavily on the ability to communicate that thought.

The language translation analogy relates quite specifically to network protocols. For example, it might seem desirable for there to be one virtual circuit protocol, to which all other virtual circuit protocols in use within an organization would be converted. However, there are a number of special features which exist in one or another protocol family to augment the basic function of the virtual circuit. If there were one standard virtual circuit protocol, it would have to support all of those special features, or else translation into that standard form and out again would cause irreversible loss of content.

In summary, this alternative has serious problems, not the least of which is the tremendous amount of programming involved. Note, however, that this alternative is labeled "standard protocols at every level." A standard protocol at a single level might still be an alternative.

Method 2: separate logical links for each protocol

An alternative approach, somewhat at the other extreme, would be to make the central network, although it was one set of links, appear as if it were several logical sets of links, each spanning the entire building complex of the organization, and each dedicated to its own protocol.

To implement this approach, all of the gateways which hook the links of the central network together would have to be programmed to understand every protocol family which the central network supported. However, it would not be necessary that the gateways know about every level of the protocols. In particular, the gateways would only need to concern themselves with the network layer and below, and most commonly used protocols contain a network layer which is sufficiently general to deal with the type of link interconnection that a typical large company or university would have to install to physically cover its property.

The problems with this approach are administrative rather than technical. Since the gateways would be maintained by a central authority, someone in that central authority would have to be responsible for knowing about the network layer of all of the protocols used, so that they could maintain the code in the gateways. Further, when a new protocol was selected for use, this person would have to learn about it and install handlers for it in every gateway. From a management point of view, taking into account the complexity of several protocol handlers trying to coexist in a single physical gateway, this approach is somewhat alarming.

Method 3:
the standard
network protocol

A third approach to solving this problem has some of the advantages and some of the defects of both of the above schemes. Method 1, which required every host implementor to provide a conversion routine between his native protocols and a standard set of protocols, was discussed and rejected. However, the discussion of Method 2 pointed out that a central network is really only concerned with protocols up through the network layer. This being the case, it might be possible to define a standard at the network level, a "standard network protocol."

The standard network protocol would define a single address space in which all of the machines on the central network would be numbered. Any two hosts wishing to communicate with each other using an existing protocol software package would need to modify that package in one small way: the vendor supplied implementation of the network layer would have to be replaced or augmented by the addition of a handler for the standard network protocol. Depending upon how the address space for the standard network protocol was defined, this change would turn out to be easy for some protocols and difficult for others.

The advantage of the standard-network-protocol approach is that it would require only one algorithm to be implemented in each gateway of the central network. This would clearly be a great reduction in the effort required to maintain the central network. However, this scheme would place an increased programming burden on all of the host maintainers. While the burden is not overwhelmingly large, it is appreciable, and many host maintainers would not or could not tolerate it. Those who had written their own protocol packages would be reluctant to modify them, and those running vendor-supported protocols would have substantial problems. In the vendor-supported case, the host maintainers would usually not have access to the original implementors of the protocol package and so would have to educate themselves in order to make the changes, which would be an expensive and time-consuming effort. Further, once the change had been made, they would no longer be running unmodified vendor code, which would make the resolution of bugs much more difficult. Furthermore, in some cases vendors refuse to release source code, so it would be impossible in those cases to make the necessary modifications. Finally, since the change would be a locally maintained one, whenever a new system release came out, it would be necessary to reintegrate the standard network protocol into the new release. This would make the maintenance burden a continual one.

There is an additional reason for host maintainers to dislike the standard-network-protocol approach. This reason has not yet been discussed and involves the concept of "native mode." For most of the protocols currently in use, there already exists a particular kind of local area network technology for which these protocols have been optimized. For these preferred network technologies, the vendors have defined a standard for how packets in the protocols should be sent over the network. One could thus say that there exists a "native mode" for the use of that network by that protocol.

Thus, the host maintainer who uses a vendor-supplied protocol package not only wants to avoid making any modifications to the package to add a standard network protocol, but also wants to use a local network technology for which his vendor has supplied a native mode. Connecting to a network for which his vendor has not defined a native mode would require that he write a new device driver in order to talk to the physical hardware, a new link level handler, and probably a new interface to the vendor's network layer. Faced with these tasks, he would probably prefer to use the vendor-supported native-mode network technology, even if it were only a serial interface, rather than modify his software.

At first glance, the desire of users to utilize a particular native mode suggests that a corporation or university would have to cover its entire property with several physical networks, so that each protocol to be supported had access to a network that represented the manufacturer-supported native mode for that protocol. If this vision were true, little would be gained from having a central network. The proponents of each type of network would install their own network, as there would be no economy of scale in centralizing the effort. Fortunately, things are not that bad. First, a number of vendors have agreed to define a native mode for common types of local area network technology such as Ethernet. Second, interest in a particular vendor's product tends to be geographically localized. Just because it is necessary to install a particular vendor's network in one building does not mean that it has to be installed in all buildings. These two factors suggest that it might be possible to create a central network that consisted of a central "spine" to which smaller networks connected via gateways. These smaller networks could consist of serial lines (the simplest case), networks for which a number of vendors had agreed upon a native mode, and vendor propietary networks.

Method 4: access networks and spine networks

As suggested above, the fourth method of achieving network support for multiple protocols consists of a central network that is a spine with a number of smaller networks which connect to the spine via gateways.

The smaller networks permit hosts to access the central spine utilizing the network technology for which the host manufacturer has defined a native mode for the protocols that are to be used. The smaller networks are referred to as "access networks."

Access networks

Unfortunately, there is no single industry standard by which a host connects to a network, and any organization which has a wide variety of hosts must support a wide variety of access networks.

The simplest and most traditional network access method is a serial line from the host to a network interface computer (which in this case functions as a gateway to the spine). Several vendors have their own internal standards for the use of a serial line for this purpose, and there is an industry standard, X.25, which many vendors support. This type of interface will become even more important as the use of personal computers grows, because a serial line is often the only communications interface available on such computers.

Another access method is the implementation of nonproprietary local network standards (such as Ethernet) to which many hosts may directly connect. A host connects to this network, not through a general-purpose serial interface, but through a special-purpose peripheral interface which has been designed for the manufacturer to connect to this particular network. Examples of such interfaces are discussed in some detail in Chapter 6.

The final form of network access is via a vendor-specific proprietary network. For some manufacturers, the features of their local area network are an integral part of their product and differentiate it from the products of other manufacturers. Because the network is deemed to provide a competitive advantage, the specifications of such network are not in the public domain, and other manufacturers are neither permitted nor encouraged to connect their hardware to these networks. Yet an organization which has purchased systems from several such vendors may wish to interconnect them in some fashion to provide common access to a resource such as a satellite ground station.

Spine networks

The various forms of access networks suggested above would all connect to the "spine network." Spine networks deal with an entirely different set of problems from those faced by access networks. While access networks would generally be deployed through a building in such a way that they are near all relevant hosts, spine networks would be used to go between buildings. They would be designed with concern for long runs through ducts, access via microwave links, and other problems related to spanning distances of several kilometers.

A spine network would not have hosts directly connected to it; all connections to the spine network would involve gateways, of which there would be two types:

1. "Access gateways," which connect the access networks to the spine network
2. "Internal gateways," which connect the various links of the spine together

The isolation of the spine network from the hosts by means of gateways provides great flexibility in installing and changing the spine network. Any type of spine link necessary to get between two points could theoretically be installed, and if it were subsequently found not to meet the network requirements, it could be replaced in a way that was invisible to the hosts since they are not directly attached. Access networks, in contrast, would be the subject of fewer changes. They would tend to have a long lifetime because their associated host installations would tend to long lifetimes, and changing an access network would require perturbation of all attached hosts and would hence be undesirable. In summary, distinguishing between access networks and spine networks gives great flexibility to incorporate growth and change the network environment without perturbing the existing software.

Spine network protocol support

An important distinction between an access net and a spine net is that on the spine net one has the option of eliminating native mode transport in favor of a standard network protocol. Since there are no hosts attached to the spine, the use of a standard network protocol does not require changes in the software in the hosts, but only changes in the software in the access gateways, where conversion between the standard network protocol used on the spine and the native mode protocols used on the access networks would occur.

Would use of a standard network protocol on the spine be a good idea? Would it be preferable to take the standard network protocol approach and incur the aforementioned protocol programming in the access gateways? Or would it be better to take the "multiprotocol spine" approach and implement a network level algorithm for each of the important protocol families in all of the internal gateways in the spine network? A number of things need to be considered in answering these questions. A discussion of addressing and of routing will give an idea of the issues involved.

Spine network addressing requirements

The fundamental purpose of the spine network is to carry packets from one access network to another. In order to accomplish this, each access gateway must have an address. When a packet is passed through an access gateway onto the spine, it will contain a protocol-specific network address that must be translated to identify the destination access gateway for the packet. The requirement for the spine addressing system is that it make this transformation from native mode addressing to spine addressing as easy as possible.

The standard-network-protocol approach solves this problem by defining a single standard spine address structure and requiring all access gateways to translate between the protocol specific address and the standard spine address. The problem with this approach is that the various native mode address structures with which the transformation must cope have drastically different architecture, so that it is very difficult to create a single spine addressing system that makes this transformation easy in every case.

The multiprotocol approach for the spine avoids the address translation problem. For each protocol that uses the spine, a separate protocol-specific address structure is created. The only difficulty with this approach occurs if the particular protocol does not have a sufficiently rich addressing structure to describe the kind of multilink addressing structure that a large spine network would require.

Spine network routing requirements

Closely related to the question of addressing is the question of routing. After an access gateway has found the address of a destination access gateway, it is then necessary to find the series of hops through the spine by which the packet should actually be transported. It would be possible to install static tables in all of the gateways, to provide a mapping between the destination address and a particular series of link addresses, but such a static table would not permit the use of backup routes if a normal route had failed. Unless the spine network (including its gateways) is extremely reliable, it seems more appropriate to use the dynamic routing strategies commonly used in modern long-haul networks.

Since the standard-network-protocol approach provides a special spine-addressing structure, a single dynamic routing algorithm can be installed in all of the gateways.

If the multiprotocol approach is used, all of the links of the spine must be assigned addresses in each of the relevant protocol structures. It would then be necessary to implement a dynamic routing algorithm for each of the protocol families.

It appears that the standard-network-protocol approach has a clear advantage here. However, the advantage of the single address space and routing algorithm is not as great as it may seem, because it would be necessary to do an implementation of each protocol's routing algorithm inside the access network gateways anyway. Given that it is necessary to build it there, it would be reasonable to deploy the same algorithm inside the internal gateways.

Other spine network requirements

In addition to the addressing and routing requirements discussed above, there are requirements such as reliability, congestion control, security, and ease of maintenance. Many of these issues, such as security, do not substantially influence the choice between a standard-network-protocol approach and a multiprotocol spine approach.

Multiprotocol spine versus standard protocol spine: conclusion

The multiprotocol spine makes life easier for the developers of the access network gateways, and is easy to understand. It does not require the development of complex algorithms to translate the features of a particular protocol into a standard network protocol. For example, when a protocol wishes to broadcast in the multiprotocol case, it does so in whatever fashion is appropriate for that protocol, and the software that handles that protocol in each of the spine network gateways makes sure that the packet gets broadcast over all of the relevant links of the spine network. Performing this same task in a standard network protocol would require the development of a complex multilink broadcast algorithm.

As discussed above, addressing is far easier in the multiprotocol case, and routing problems involve roughly equivalent work. Problems will arise, however, in dealing with a protocol that is deficient in its addressing, routing, or other functions. Furthermore, problems may arise fitting the required protocol handlers into the gateway machines. These machines should have at least 24 bits of addressing capability.

The multiprotocol spine approach should be adopted unless the number of protocols to be supported grows too large or changes too rapidly. The limits for "too large" or "too rapidly" are based on administrative complexity (getting the spine network gateway software changed) and on space within the gateway. Neither of these limits is clearly understood.

Providing multiprotocol network services

In Chapter 9, a number of network services were described, including print services, file services, and backup services. The protocols to support such services in a single-vendor network are usually provided by the vendor. Even in a small network that supports hardware and software from multiple vendors, the problem of protocols is still manageable. However, in large networks, such as those discussed in this chapter, it is difficult to provide network services to the various users of the network, since they program their machines in different protocols.

One approach would be for the organization providing the services to select a protocol family as its standard and to require that any client of the service must implement that family on his machine. This would be similar to the previously discussed case of a central network whose gateways handle only one protocol, and again a programming burden would be shifted from the service supplier to the service user. If there is a strong consensus that one protocol should be supported by almost all of the machines on the network, this approach is workable. However, if there are a large number of machines from differing vendors with differing protocol packages, then this scheme is unworkable in its purest form and a fall-back approach must be taken. The fall-back approach is to have separate service providers for the service user groups utilizing various vendor machines.

A second approach would be for the centralized services to be made available using a number of different protocols, so that a variety of vendors' machines could be clients of these services without implementing new protocol software. If this could be done without an overwhelming effort by the organization providing the services, it would clearly be the better strategy. Unfortunately, while the application levels of many protocols contain specifications for a few services such as remote log-in, many services such as storage or high-quality printing are often unspecified.

A third approach would be for the corporation or college providing the network to develop its own protocols for network services. These protocols would be at the application level and would be designed to operate over the transport layer of any of the protocol families in use on the network.

Terminal support

In addition to providing connections between computers and network services, a local area network must also support simple terminals ("dumb terminals"). The use of terminal concentrators to provide this support was discussed briefly in Chapter 9, but without exploring the problems of multiple protocol support that are the hallmark of the large networks dealt with in this chapter.

While many people anticipate that the simple terminal will be superseded by personal computers, it seems likely that a substantial number of such terminals will be connected to networks for many years to come. Thus, networks will have to provide connections between terminals and hosts, a type of connection that is substantially different than a connection between hosts.

Computers are programmed with special software to speak one or more protocols, but terminals are not. Terminals expect to transmit and receive ASCII (usually) characters as serial bit streams through a standard RS-232-C (or RS-422 or RS-423) plug. Thus, if terminals are to be connected to a local area network, they must be connected through an interface computer which has been programmed to speak the necessary protocols on behalf of the terminals.

There are two stages in a typical connection from a terminal to a host computer over a network. The first stage is the connection from the terminal to a network interface computer which typically serves a number of terminals, and is hence called a terminal concentrator. The second stage is the connection from the concentrator to the host. There are several approaches to each of these stages.

The first stage, terminal to concentrator, is often solved by putting the concentrator physically next to the terminal, so that a permanent wire can be installed to connect the two. This has the benefit of bringing the local area network wiring into the office areas, and the future addition of high-speed workstations that need direct connections to the network can be facilitated. However, it also has the drawback, in a large organization, that a large number of small terminal concentrators (four to eight lines, for example) must be deployed to make sure that one is close enough to each present or planned terminal location. The alternative is to build larger terminal concentrators and install them in telephone equipment closets using twisted pair wiring to connect between terminals and the concentrators. Alternatively, the concentrators could be completely centralized and some type of telecommunications equipment could be used to connect the terminals to the concentrator.

The second stage, from concentrator to host, can be achieved in a variety of ways. A very simple approach, which requires no software modification to the host, is to place a "reverse concentrator" next to each host. Such a device connects to the network on one side and provides a large number of serial line connections on the other side. The serial line connections are cabled to conventional local terminal multiplexers on the host machine. Because of the appearance of cables running from the reverse concentrator to the host, this has been called the "milking machine" approach to terminal support. This approach is quite adequate (although expensive) for connecting terminals to hosts, but the reverse concentrator provides none of the requirements for host-to-host communications, and thus additional hardware and software would be necessary for that purpose.

A more sophisticated alternative is to add new network software to the host, and allow the concentrator and the host to establish direct network connections. This has several advantages over the previous approach. First, it eliminates the necessity for the reverse concentrator and all of the serial interface gear associated with it. Second, directly connecting the host to the network allows the same network connection to be used for terminal support, remote log-in support, host-to-host network connections, and the other network services. The problem with the direct network connection approach is that it brings back the problem of which protocol family should be used. Many hosts already come equipped with software to support remote log-in and other services, provided that the concentrator speaks the correct protocol family. Once again, the lack of a single protocol standard means that remote log-in must have a multiprotocol requirement if it is to be generally useful.

If concentrators are physically distributed so that the decision about which concentrator to use is determined by where the user is physically located, rather than by which protocol the user wishes to use, the concentrators must be capable of supporting multiple protocols, because the person at a terminal connected to a concentrator might want to use any of several protocols depending on which host he wanted to use.

An alternative would be to provide a physically centralized pool of concentrators, each speaking a particular protocol, to which terminals were connected by a terminal switching mechanism. A terminal switching facility could also be used to provide the serial access which is the only communications option for many personal computers, especially those being used from homes or remote sites.

Summary

For a large organization such as a multibuilding business complex or a university, the installation of dozens of local area networks can cause problems. The installation of a single local area network to span the entire property is also frequently infeasible. The best solution may well lie in a centrally administered spine network to which various local area networks interconnect by means of access gateways. The spine network, the services provided on a network-wide basis, and the terminal concentrators used to connect simple terminals to the network should offer multiple protocol support to the maximum extent possible, but a number of alternative strategies should also be considered.

Reference

Clark, David D. *M.I.T. Campus Network Implementation Planning Document.* M.I.T. Laboratory for Computer Science CCNG-2, Cambridge, Mass., June 1983.

12   Standards

Local area networks have created a tremendous need for standards, as such networks typically involve shared access to services such as compilation, filing, printing, and communications. These services are both shared among users and distributed among multiple machines. To further complicate the problem, the services and the machines upon which they operate are often provided by a diverse collection of hardware and software vendors. In addition, the networks that contain such a diverse collection of users and services often have a need to be linked together, as was discussed in Chapter 11.

Link and physical layer standards

The standards activity in local area networks began at the physical and data link levels of the ISO layered model. One of the first cases of multiple vendors agreeing upon a standard in this area was the Ethernet Specification. Digital Equipment Corporation, Intel Corporation, and Xerox Corporation agreed to Version 1.0 of this standard on 30 September 1980. Since that time, a new revision, Version 2.0, has been agreed to by these companies. This document can be obtained by writing to:

Digital Equipment Corporation
444 Whitney Street
Northboro, MA 01532

and requesting publication AA–K759B–TK.

Beginning in 1980, the Institute of Electrical and Electronics Engineers (IEEE) began work on IEEE Standard 802, a family of standards for local area networks. An introductory document, Standard 802.1, describes the relationship of the various standards in the 802 family and relates them to the ISO model described in Chapter 8 of this book. In addition, 802.1 explains the relationship between the 802 protocols and higher-level protocols, discussing issues associated with interconnecting and managing networks in the process. The other 802 family documents are related as shown in Figure 53.

The 802 family of standards includes four combinations of network topologies and access methods:

Standard	Description
802.3	A bus utilizing CSMA/CD
802.4	A bus utilizing token passing
802.5	A ring utilizing token passing
802.6	A metropolitan area network

Copies of these standards may be purchased by writing to:

IEEE Computer Society Order Department
10662 Los Vagueros Circle
Los Alamitos, CA 90702

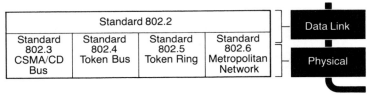

*Figure 53. IEEE 802 standards
in relation to ISO protocols*

Standards above the link layer

Standards above the link layer of the ISO model have been primarily "standards" only within the product offerings of a particular vendor. For example, IBM offers SNA (Systems Network Architecture), Xerox offers XNS (Xerox Network Services), and Digital Equipment offers DNA (Digital Network Architecture). In some cases, other vendors have adopted protocols that closely resemble these, so they are multivendor "standards" to some degree.

One organization which has developed standards that truly transcend the boundaries between various vendor products has been the Defense Advanced Research Projects Agency (DARPA, widely referred to by its old acronym, ARPA). Starting with an experimental four-node network in late 1969, the ARPANET has grown more than a hundredfold, as has the world's knowledge of networks, largely thanks to the research conducted on the ARPANET.

The first transport level protocol used on ARPANET was called NCP (Network Control Protocol) and assumed that the lower levels (network, data link, and physical) delivered error-free messages in correct order. While this assumption was reasonable at the time, subsequent ARPANET research involved connections to unreliable networks, and a more sophisticated transport level protocol was required. The new protocol, the result of several years of effort, was called TCP (Transmission Control Protocol) and included a new network layer protocol referred to as the internet protocol, or IP. The combination of these transport and network level protocols is referred to as TCP/IP and has been a Department of Defense standard since about 1978. It was officially adopted on a network-wide basis on 1 January 1983.

The International Organization for Standardization (ISO) is now developing standard network protocols for the various layers in the ISO reference model. Many of these standards are in at least draft form. In the United States, the National Bureau of Standards (NBS) is also supporting the development of standard network protocols and has developed test tools which should significantly reduce the risk of incompatibilities in multivendor networks based on the ISO protocols.

Copies of the ISO standards, and many other standards of interest, may be obtained by writing to:

American National Standards Institute (ANSI)
1430 Broadway
New York, NY 10018

A word of caution

Standards writing is a very difficult business. If a technology is relatively mature, it may be too late for standards. Each company offering a product will have developed certain tricks and features in its hardware and software which it feels provide a competitive advantage. Agreement to a standard may force the company to either abandon those "value added" features or reveal the details thereof to their competitors. Worse than that, if a really useful standard is to be created, the features and tricks will have to be made available to everyone.

The above reasoning would suggest that standards are best developed before anyone has any hardware or software on the market. While this reduces the provincialism displayed at the standards meetings, the meeting attendees may find themselves with the opposite problem—the details of implementation are unknown. After a standard is agreed upon, the various parties go out and implement a product according to their interpretation of the standard. Regardless of how carefully the standard was written, there will be slight inconsistencies in implementation, especially in those areas where the standards committee members did not fully understand the technology. Some of the inconsistencies will be reconciled, but some will not. Therefore, it behooves a purchaser of local area network components to advise a potential supplier what network components are already in place and ask for a guarantee that the about-to-be-purchased parts will interoperate with the existing devices. This may have to be accomplished by borrowing or purchasing a limited number of the new units and performing experiments. While one might hope that truly comprehensive standards and truly effective compliance therewith will soon obviate the need for such guarantees and tests, it seems likely that caution will be required at least through the remainder of the 1980s.

Reference   Tanenbaum, Andrew S. *Computer Networks*. Englewood Cliffs, N.J.: Prentice Hall, 1981.

Glossary

access methods   Techniques for determining which of several stations that desire to transmit will be the next to use a shared transmission medium.

access network   A local area network, generally very limited in geographical coverage, that allows users to communicate among each other and also permits access to a "spine network" that covers a larger distance and interconnects several access networks. An access network is often used to interconnect computer equipment provided by the same vendor or equipment that was designed to function optimally on that type of network.

address   A grouping of numbers that uniquely identifies a station in a local area network, or a location in computer memory, or a house on a street, etc. For a local area network station or a computer memory location, electronic logic can be arranged to ignore messages not bearing the appropriate address and accept messages that do bear the appropriate address.

address field   A section of a message, generally at the beginning, in which the address of the intended receiving station is found.

address space   A measure of the amount of memory that can be installed on a computer. A computer that utilizes 24 bits to designate a memory location is said to have a 24-bit address space; it can address twice as much memory as a computer having a 23-bit address space.

algorithm   A set of rules for accomplishing a task. A repeated sequence of steps that a device or program executes to accomplish the task for which it was designed.

ALOHA   A computer network serving the Hawaiian islands that utilized radio transmission for data communications. Because individual stations could only hear a master station and could not hear one another, a station desiring to transmit did so whenever it pleased. The "transmit at will" system of accessing a transmission medium is referred to as an ALOHA system in honor of this pioneering computer network.

alternate buffer   In a data communications device, a section of memory set aside for the transmission or reception of data. When that section of memory is empty (transmission) or full (reception), data transmission over a communications line continues using the "primary buffer," while the associated computer transfers data to or from the alternate buffer in anticipation of its use when the primary buffer is empty or full.

analog signal   An electrical signal that can assume any of an infinite number of voltage or current values, in contrast to a digital signal, which can assume only one of a finite number of values. For example, a signal that could assume any value of voltage between 0 and 4 volts (such as 1.2837465954 . . .) would be an analog signal. If a signal could assume only the values 0 volts, 1 volt, 2 volts, or 3 volts, such a signal would be a digital signal and could be represented by the binary (digital) values 00, 01, 10, and 11.

application level   The highest protocol level in the *ISO layered model* of data communications protocols. This is the level that actually performs a service for the user, for example a mail service.

ARPA   Advanced Research Projects Agency, an agency of the U.S. Defense Department. It is now referred to as DARPA, the Defense Advanced Research Projects Agency.

ARPANET   A network of computers, located principally at U.S. univerities (but with many other connections, including overseas). This network has been in use since the 1960s and has been the site of many advances in computer communications. It has been sponsored by ARPA.

ASCII   The American Standard Code for Information Interchange.

availability   A measure of how often a person who wants to use a computer system finds that the system is available for use. Contrast with *reliability*.

AWG   American wire gauge, a method of expressing the size of electrical wires. The numbering system is inversely proportional to the physical cross section of the wire. For example, heavy industrial wiring may use #0 or #2. Homes are wired with #12 or #14. Telephone systems use #22, #24, or #26.

babbling tributary   A station that continuously transmits meaningless messages.

back-off   The process of delaying an attempt to transmit. A station customarily backs off when an earlier attempt to transmit met with some difficulty, such as encountering a collision in a CSMA/CD system.

backplane bus   A collection of electrical wiring that interconnects the slots where modules in a computer system are inserted. The backplane bus wiring connects the same signal to identically numbered pins of each module in the computer system. For example, the "reset" signal might be connected to pin 22 of each module via the backplane bus wiring.

backup server   A program that administers the copying of users' files so that at least two up-to-date copies always exist.

bandwidth   The measure of a transmission facility's ability to transmit signals that span a range of frequencies without degrading the amount of power in the signal more than some percentage (usually 50 percent). For example, if measurements are performed on a transmission line and it is found that all signals of frequency below 300 Hz and all signals of frequency beyond 3000 Hz lose half their power traversing the line, while signals between 300 and 3000 Hz retain at least 50 percent of their power, the line is said to have a bandwidth of 2700 Hz (3000−300).

baseband A transmission system in which signals are applied to the transmission medium without being translated in frequency. For example, human voice signals in the 300–3000 Hz range would occur on the transmission facility in the 300–3000 Hz range. In a baseband system, there is typically only a single set of signals present on the transmission medium. Contrast with *broadband*.

batch system A computer system in which a user submits a program for execution and later receives an indication as to whether or not it ran successfully. Typically, the program awaited its turn to run and ran to completion without other programs intervening. Contrast with *timesharing*.

binary Relating to a number system that allows only two values, 0 and 1. Also, relating to a numeric quantity expressed solely in 0s and 1s.

BISYNC Binary synchronous protocol, a system that IBM developed in the early 1960s for transmitting data over synchronous data communications facilities. It utilizes special characters and special character sequences to indicate what portions of a message are the header, the data, and the frame check sequence. Special character sequences are also used to indicate the beginning and end of messages, "turn around" half duplex lines, and recover from error situations.

bit A binary unit of information that can have either of two states, 0 or 1. In contrast, a decimal digit can have any of ten values, 0, 1, 2, 3, 4, 5, 6, 7, 8, or 9.

bit bucket A slang term used to describe the discard of binary information by relating it to the practice of throwing paper or other information into a wastebasket or bucket.

bit buffer A storage element capable of storing a single binary unit (bit) of information.

blocking A condition in a switching system in which a call cannot be processed because control equipment or transmission paths are not available.

booting The process of loading a computer's memory with sufficient information that it can function. Often, the first information loaded is used by the computer to read in additional information, a process akin to "pulling oneself up by one's bootstraps," hence the term *bootstrapping* or *booting*.

bps Bits per second, a measure of transmission speed.

bridge A device used to expand a local area network by forwarding frames between data link layers associated with two different kinds of physical link. Also called a data link relay or level 2 relay.

broadband   A transmission system in which signals are applied to the transmission medium after being translated in frequency. For example, human voice signals in the 300–3000 Hz range might occur on the transmission facility in the 2,000,300–2,003,000 Hz range. In a broadband system, there are typically many different sets of signals on the transmission medium at one time, each set of signals having been translated to other noninterfering frequencies. In local area network usage, *broadband* refers to systems that handle many simultaneous signals and use CATV hardware to distribute the signals. Contrast with *baseband.*

broadcast medium   A transmission system in which all messages are heard by all stations.

broadcast message   A message addressed to all users of a computer network.

buffered   A message that has been buffered is one that has been stored, typically in semiconductor memory located in network controller logic.

buffering requirements   The amount of memory locations required to store messages.

bus   A local area network topology in which all stations attach to a single transmission medium so that all stations are equal and all stations hear all transmissions on the medium. *Bus* is also used as an abbreviation for *backplane bus* in some applications.

bus hog   A method of operating direct memory access (DMA) devices in which the device obtains control of the backplane bus and remains in control until it has completed as many data transfers as it desires.

bus segment   A section or piece of bus that is electrically continuous, with no intervening components such as repeaters. Electrical continuity may be maintained using fixtures such as coaxial cable connectors, but no signal boosting equipment may intervene. If signal boosting equipment (repeaters) are used, the piece of cable on the other side of such equipment is defined as another bus segment.

bus topology   See *bus.*

busy hour   A sixty-minute period during the busiest day of the year during which a switching system receives the greatest demand for service.

bypass relays   Relays in a ring network that permit message traffic to travel between two nodes that are not normally adjacent. Usually, such relays are arranged so that any node can be removed from the ring for servicing and the two nodes on either side of the removed node are now connected via the bypass relay.

byte count   The number of 8-bit quantities in a message. Since ASCII characters can be encoded in 8 bits, the byte count is also called the "character count." Byte count is also used to describe the set of protocols that use character counting to designate which portions of a message are the header, data, and frame check sequence. See *DDCMP.*

byte   A group of eight bits.

carrier   A (usually) continuous sinusoidal signal, applied to a communications medium, which does not convey information until altered in some fashion, such as having its amplitude changed (amplitude modulation), its frequency changed (frequency modulation), or its phase changed (phase modulation). The changes convey the information.

carrier detect circuitry   Electronic components arranged to detect the presence of a carrier signal and thus detect that a transmission medium is in use and/or that data is being transmitted.

cassette tape   A rather slow-speed and low-capacity method of storing data using the same general technology as audio cassettes.

CATV   Community antenna television, a method of delivering quality television reception by taking signals from a well-situated central antenna and delivering them to people's homes by means of a coaxial cable network. The electrical components for such systems can also be used to create broadband local area networks.

CCS   Hundred (Roman numeral C) call seconds, a unit of traffic intensity in switching systems. One hundred calls present for a second, or one call present for 100 seconds, equals one CCS of traffic. A call present for 3600 seconds (36 CCS) is a call present for an hour, which equals one Erlang of traffic.

circuit switching   A method of allowing telephones or data stations to establish a connection on a temporary basis. When the connection has been established, the two stations appear to be connected by a piece of wire, as the full bandwidth of the wire used to reach the switching system is available between the stations, and there is no noticeable delay in the transission of voice or data between the stations.

channel banks   Collections of electronic circuitry used at each end of time-division-multiplex transmission systems to divide the available bandwidth in the transmission system into separate channels and to provide control of those channels.

coaxial cable   A type of electrical cable in which a piece of wire is surrounded by insulation and then surrounded by a tubular piece of metal whose axis of curvature coincides with the center of the piece of wire, hence the term *coaxial*.

collision   Simultaneous transmission over a transmission medium in a way that produces unusable data.

collision detection   The process of detecting that simultaneous interfering transmission has taken place. Typically, each transmitting station that detects the collision will wait some period of time and try again.

common carrier   An organization licensed to provide a specific set of services for a specific set of rates, as delineated in an agreed-upon document called a tariff. Generally, the organization will be using a resource such as highways, airways, or rights-of-way in which the public interest is best served by limiting access to the resource by means of the licensing process. In exchange for receiving the license, the organization agrees to serve all customers fairly and charge only the designated rates.

common file system A combination of hardware and software that provides all users of a network with access to the same information. The ability to update the information may be given to all users or may be limited to a privileged few. In either case, all users have access to the information as soon as it is updated.

computation server A computer of moderate to high performance attached to a local area network for the purpose of providing network users with such services as matrix inversion or other computation-intensive tasks.

comparator An electrical circuit that can compare the numerical value of two quantities, A and B. The circuit will then assert one of three signals: A greater than B, A equal to B, A less than B.

compilation The translation of programs written in a language understandable to programmers into instructions understandable to the computer.

connector (token ring) A pattern of bits that signifies the boundary between two messages. Typically, the connector is similar to the token, but with one bit changed. A station wishing to transmit withdraws the token from the end of the message string on the ring, alters the token to form a connector, adds its message, and then inserts a token.

contact bounce An imperfection in relay switching caused by the physical properties of relay contacts. When two contacts close, they may touch each other with sufficient force that the contacts move apart and then strike again. This process may take place for several milliseconds. One solution to the problem is to coat the contacts with mercury, which will form a conductive coating that will bridge the contacts together during the bouncing period.

contention A method of having multiple stations access a transmission medium by having each station decide, on an equal basis with other stations, when it will transmit. This method is in contrast with methods in which a master station tells other stations when they may transmit and methods in which a permission-to-transmit token is passed from station to station.

CPU Central processing unit, that part of a computer in which mathematical operations are performed.

CRC See *cyclic redundancy check*.

crossbar A type of electromechanical telephone switching system invented in the early twentieth century and perfected in midcentury. The name comes from the placement of bar-shaped parts at ninety-degree angles in a cross pattern. The operation of one bar moves a flexible metal finger in front of several sets of contacts, and operation of the second bar presses one of the fingers against a selected set of contacts, closing them and holding them closed until the second bar (only) is released.

crosstalk | The introduction of signals from one communication channel into another.

CSMA/CD | Carrier Sense Multiple Access with Collision Detection, a method of having multiple stations access a transmission medium (multiple access) by listening until no signals are detected (carrier sense), then transmitting and checking to see if more than one signal is present (collision detection).

cyclic redundancy check | A method of detecting errors in a message by performing an involved mathematical calculation on the bits in the message and then sending the results of the calculation at the end of the message. The receiving station performs the same calculation on the message data as it is being received and then checks its result against that transmitted at the end of the message.

DARPA | Defense Advanced Research Projects Agency, a funding agency for the computer networking experiments performed over the "ARPANET."

data base | A collection of data, generally on the same subject, stored in computer-readable form, and usually indexed or arranged in some other logical order. Computer or network users can use the index or logical arrangement to find a particular item of data that they desire.

data late | A failure condition in rotating media such as disks, in which the proper part of the disk is positioned under the read/write heads for a data transfer, but the control logic is not prepared to transfer the data. Since the disk must continue to rotate, the data transfer must be delayed for a complete disk revolution time, a very severe consequence.

data link level | The second level of the *ISO layered model* of communications protocols. The first level (physical level) performs the service of delivering data to this level, and this level performs the service of collecting the data into frames, for the benefit of higher levels.

data link relay | See *bridge*.

datagram | A method of transmitting messages in which sections of the message are allowed to be transmitted through the transmission system in scattered order and the correct order is reestablished by the receiving station. Contrast with *virtual circuit*.

DC voltages | Electrical signals sent at a constant level that is always positive (or always negative) relative to earth potential, in contrast to AC voltages, which continuously vary in equal amounts on either side of earth potential.

DDCMP | Digital Data Communications Message Protocol. In this data link layer protocol, message headers contain a character count indicating the size of the message. This permits the transmission of arbitrary character sequences in the message without concern that some may be interpreted as control sequences. The protocol may be used in serial or parallel, asynchronous, or synchronous transmission.

decoding
: In digital telephony, the process of converting digital signals to analog signals, especially the process of converting digitized speech to recognizable speech.

demodulate
: The process of separating a data signal from a carrier signal. A carrier signal is a continuous sinusoidal signal, applied to a communications medium, which does not convey information until altered in some fashion, such as having its amplitude changed, its frequency changed, or its phase changed. The changes convey the information, and the demodulation process detects what those changes were.

destination address
: That part of a message which indicates for whom the message is intended.

diagnostic
: A program for operating an electronic device over a range of operating conditions and input data patterns, similar to (or more extreme than) those the device is likely to encounter in normal use. The program compares the results obtained with the known correct answers and reports discrepancies. The diagnostic can also be arranged to repeat a particular test until failure occurs, or repeat a failing test so that measurement apparatus can be attached to various portions of the failing device.

differential transmission
: A method of transmitting data in which a signal is sent upon two wires in such a fashion that the information conveyed is the difference in voltage between the two wires. The two wires are run twisted about each other such that each is equally subject to interference. If the interference occurs on each wire equally, the effects of the interference will be canceled when the receiver subtracts one wire's voltage from that of the other, yet the information (the difference between the voltages) will be revealed in the subtraction process.

digital data
: Information transmitted as discrete electrical quantities, for example as signals representing zeros and ones, rather than as a continuum of voltages.

digital switching
: In telephony, the practice of encoding analog voice samples into digital data and routing the data through logic circuitry in much the same fashion as a computer. Like a computer, digital switching systems are fast, compact, and economical, and require less maintenance than comparable electromechanical systems.

digital transmission
: In telephony, the practice of encoding analog voice samples into digital data, transmitting that data, and reconstructing (decoding) the analog voice samples at the receiving end. Digital transmission has the benefit of being less sensitive to noise than analog transmission, since only two states of information, 0 and 1, need be sent. In addition, digital data can be regenerated rather than amplified, preventing noise from being amplified along with the signal, as it would be in analog transmission.

disk server
: A computer system equipped with disks and a program that permits network users to create and store files on the disks. The persons creating the files can read and write data in their own portion of the disk. Controlled sharing of access to files is usually limited or nonexistent. Contrast with *file server*.

distributed PBX A private branch exchange whose switching equipment is divided into small elements located at various points in a building and interconnected by a local area network. In a typical system, each element is capable of handling 128 lines and is located in an equipment closet within a few hundred feet of the telephones being served. A distributed PBX is in contrast to a conventional PBX, in which wiring from all of the telephones served goes to a single central switch.

DMA Direct memory access, which describes circuitry that enables a device such as a disk, tape, or communications interface to deposit data directly into a computer memory without the assistance of the central processing unit (CPU).

DNA Digital Network Architecture, Digital Equipment Corporation's layered data communications protocols.

down-line loading A system in which programs are loaded into the memory of a computer system via the same communications line(s) that the system normally uses to communicate with the rest of a network. This system is in contrast to systems in which all programs are loaded into the computer from a disk or tape associated with the computer.

drop In telephony, the wiring from the telephone pole to a person's home. In networks, the wiring unique to a particular user.

duct system Tubular enclosures that hold wires and cables and enable them to pass through the floors of a building or between buildings.

dumb terminal A keyboard and screen or keyboard and printer that convey data generated by the user's keystrokes directly to a computer or network without buffering or otherwise acting upon the data. Data traveling from the computer to the user are also not processed in any fashion other than to transfer them to the display device.

duty cycle The relationship between the time a device is on and the time it is off. For example, a heater that is on for one hour a day is said to have a low duty cycle.

dynamic routing strategy A technique for directing messages through a network in which the rules used for which messages go where, by what path, can be changed "on the fly" as circumstances (such as congestion areas) change.

ECL Emitter coupled logic, a design style of transistor circuits used in computers and characterized by fast operation and high heat dissipation.

encoding In telephony, the practice of encoding analog voice samples into digital data. This is typically done by picking 255 voltage levels, assigning each an 8-bit binary number. The voltage level of the samples is compared with the 255 voltage levels and the nearest level is chosen. The 8-bit number for that voltage level is then sent.

Erlang	A measure of telephone traffic intensity named after A. K. Erlang, an employee of the British Post Office in the early 1900s who was a pioneer in telephone traffic theory. An Erlang is the occupancy of a circuit for one hour.
error detection	The process of performing a mathematical operation upon the data sent and sending the results of that operation along with the data. The receiving station performs the same operation and compares its result with that sent. The operation may be a simple indication of whether the number of 1s in some part of the message is even or odd; the operation may also be much more complicated.
Ethernet	A CSMA/CD system, utilizing coaxial cable, developed at Xerox Corporation's Palo Alto Research Center. This system is described in an article by R. M. Metcalfe and D. R. Boggs in the *Communications of the ACM*, July 1976. The initial systems ran at 3 MHz; the system commercialized by Xerox, Intel, and Digital Equipment runs at 10 MHz.
exchange	The official telephone company definition is "An area over which telephone service is provided by one switching system, or by multiple switching systems treated as a single system for rate-making purposes." In common usage, a telephone switching system.
exponential backoff	In *CSMA/CD*, the practice of waiting a random period of time after each collision encountered, and increasing the mean of the random numbers used by a factor of 2 after each successive collision encountered.
fiber optics	A data transmission medium consisting of fine glass fibers. Light-emitting diodes introduce light into one end of the fiber, and it bounces off the inside of the surface of the fiber until it reaches the other end, where a detector converts the light back into an electrical signal. There are also varieties of fiber, called graded index fibers, in which the light is bent back toward the center when it gets near the surface of the fiber, rather than actually bouncing off the inside of the surface.
file	An ordered collection of data, usually stored on a disk or tape and associated with or created by a particular person.
file server	A computer system equipped with disks or tapes and a program that permits network users to create and store files on the disks or tapes. The persons creating the files can allow other network users to read the files, to read and write in the files, or to have no access at all. Contrast with *disk server.*
filter	An electronic circuit that allows signals within a given frequency range to pass through the circuit without loss, while suppressing signals outside that range.
firmware	Programs kept in semipermanent storage, such as various types of read-only memory; such programs can be altered, but with difficulty. Contrast with *hardware* and *software.*
flag	A program-readable indicator signifying that data are available, that space is available to store data, or that some operation has been completed. The name

derives from rural mailboxes in which a metal flag indicates that the letter carrier should pick up mail from the homeowner, or that the homeowner should pickup mail from the letter carrier. Also, in HDLC and SDLC data link protocols, a distinctive bit pattern (01111110) that indicates the beginning and end of frames.

floppy disk A flexible plastic disk coated with magnetic material and used to store data. These disks are noted for their economy, ease of handling, and slow speed.

flow control Hardware or software mechanisms employed in data communications to turn off transmission when the receiving station is unable to store the data it is receiving.

formats Ways of arranging data in a message in prescribed order so that a receiving station knows where to find special information within the message.

frame check sequence Another name for cyclic redundancy check.

frame A group of bits, the first several bits being a "header" containing address and other control information, the next bits being the data being conveyed, and the last bits being a check sequence for error detection.

framing In transmission, the process of dividing data that is to be transmitted into groups of bits and adding a header and a check sequence to form a frame (see *frame*). In reception, the process of recognizing which groups of incoming bits constitute frames. In both transmission and reception, the framing process is accomplished by the data link layer of a protocol family following the ISO layered model.

full duplex The capability of transmitting in both directions simultaneously.

gateway In local area networks, a computer system and its associated software that permit two networks using different protocols to communicate with each other. A gateway translates all protocol levels from physical layer up through applications layer, and can thus be used to interconnect networks that differ in every detail.

graphics station A collection of hardware and software that features a high-resolution video display that presents information to the user in the form of both text and images. An input device that responds to the movement of the user's hand, in addition to a keyboard, is often provided.

Grosch's Law The amount of computational power obtained rises as the square of the price paid. First stated by Herbert Grosch.

guard band In the allocation of frequencies for radio broadcast, broadband cable systems, or modems, a set of unused frequencies allocated in between the frequencies being used. The unused frequencies are required because *filters* are not precise enough to allow reception (or transmission) of signals on adjacent frequencies without interference.

hard copy	Printed information, as opposed to information displayed on a video screen.
hardware	Computers, printers, disks, and other devices whose fundamental characteristics were determined at the time of manufacture. Changes in such devices require the use of tools. Contrast with *firmware* and *software*.
HDLC	Hierarchical Data Link Control, a data link layer protocol in which data is transmitted with a zero inserted after each consecutive group of five 1s, except for a distinctive "flag" pattern (01111110), which delineates the beginning and end of a frame. This protocol is very similar to *SDLC*, but the header is arranged to allow for longer addresses and longer message numbers.
headend	In a CATV system, apparatus located near the receiving antenna and used to amplify and otherwise condition the received signals for transmission over the cabling system to subscribers' homes. In a broadband local area network utilizing a single cable, apparatus that translates the frequencies used for transmission of data onto the cable into the frequencies used for reception of data from the cable. In a broadband local area network utilizing two cables, a loop of cable that connects the cable used for transmission of data to the cable used for reception of data.
header	That portion of a message, at the beginning, which contains destination address, source address, message numbering, and other control information.
Hertz (Hz)	A unit of frequency equal to one cycle per second. Named in honor of Heinrich Hertz.
host	A computer system that provides computational services for a number of users.
hundred call seconds	See *CCS*.
hybrid network	A local area network employing a mixture of topologies and access methods. For example, a network that includes both a token ring and a CSMA/CD bus.
idling signal	Any signal applied to a communications line that indicates that no data is being sent. Such a signal is often used to reassure receiving stations that the line is still electrically intact and, in systems that recover clocking information from data, to keep the clock recovery circuits prepared for the arrival of data.
IEEE	The Institute of Electrical and Electronic Engineers, an information exchange, publishing, and standards-making body responsible for many standards used in local area networks, notably the 802 series.
impedance	An electrical property similar to resistance, but varying with frequency.
impedance discontinuity	A point at which the electrical properties of a transmission medium change, either because the medium itself has changed (different type of cable, for example) or because additional devices or sections of cable have been joined to the medium at that point. A change in impedance is important because when

an electrical signal arrives at the point where the change occurs, a portion of that signal's energy will be reflected back in the direction from which the signal arrived, possibly causing a malfunction.

interpacket gap The time between the conclusion of the transmission (or reception) of one packet and the transmission (or reception) of the next.

intermediate system Another name for *router*.

interrupt A signal given to a computer that, when acknowledged, causes the computer to stop what it was doing (storing the details thereof) and turn its attention to the device asserting the signal. After the device has been serviced, the computer will recover the status information concerning the previous task and will resume its execution.

interworking unit Another name for *gateway*.

IP Internetwork Protocol, a network layer protocol used on the ARPANET.

ISO The International Organization for Standardization, a standards body. This organization has developed standards for pin assignments in data communication plugs, has promulgated the layered model of communications protocols, and has specified and approved protocols for many of the layers in the layered model.

ISO layered model A way of thinking about communications protocols that models them as existing in seven layers, each layer performing services for the layers above it. The seven layers (from lowest to highest) are physical, data link, network, transport, session, presentation, and application.

kbps Kilo (1000) bits per second.

late collision A failure condition in a CSMA/CD system in which a station begins a transmission during a transmission by another station, and does so more than two *round-trip times* after the other station began its transmission. This condition can occur if the second station is unable to detect carrier from the first station's transmission or if the transmission medium is longer than it should be.

layered protocols Protocols designed to obtain services from, and deliver services to, other protocols in the fashion described by the *ISO layered model*.

level 1 relay Another name for *repeater*.

level 2 relay Another name for *bridge*.

level 3 relay Another name for *router*.

level 7 relay Another name for *gateway*.

line driver A circuit designed to transmit data outside the enclosure of a computer system, but not more than a few hundred feet. The data are not modulated or changed in any fashion, but rather higher voltage and current levels are used than would be used within a computer system.

linked list
: A system of organizing data with a computer memory; it is often used for the storage of data communication messages and is characterized by the storage of both data and the address of the next block of data. Contrast with systems which alternate between two buffers, the *primary buffer* and the *alternate buffer*.

linked list header
: A block of information indicating (1) the address of the next linked list header, (2) the address of the message text buffer, (3) the size of the message text buffer, and (4) control bits indicating special actions to be taken before or during the transmission of the text.

local area network
: A data communications network that spans a physically limited area (generally less than a mile or two), provides high-bandwidth communication over inexpensive media (generally coaxial cable or twisted pair), provides a switching capability, and is usually owned by the user (i.e., not provided by a common carrier).

log-in
: The process of identifying and authenticating (via password) oneself to a computer system.

logic levels
: The voltages used with computers to convey digital information, usually between 0.4 and 3.0 volts DC.

logic signaling levels
: See *logic levels*.

logical address
: A grouping of numbers that identifies one or more stations in a local area network that can accomplish the same class of tasks or are in some other way similar.

long line driver
: A circuit designed to transmit data outside the enclosure of a computer system, but not more than a few thousand feet. The data are not modulated or changed in any fashion, but rather higher voltage and current levels are used than would be used within a computer system or over short distances.

loop resistance
: The resistance of a wire that runs from point A to point B and back to point A. In telephone systems, the resistance of wiring from the switching system to the subscriber's telephone and back.

LSI
: Large-scale integration, the art of putting tens of thousands of transistors into a single integrated circuit, typically a quarter-inch square.

Mbps
: Mega (million) bits per second.

mail server
: A computer system and associated software that offer an electronic service analogous to that provided by a national postal service. Users may send or forward electronic mail messages to anyone else served by the system and accumulate messages in a "mailbox."

medium
: A person, mechanism, electronic pathway, or other means of conveying information from one point to another.

megabit per second
: One million bits per second.

message	An ordered collection of data that is intelligible to the sender and to the recipient.
message numbering	A method of ensuring that messages are in correct order at the receiving station, for detecting lost messages, for acknowledging the reception of correct messages (see *cyclic redundancy check*), and for requesting the retransmission of specific messages that were damaged in transit or lost.
metropolitan area network	A data communications network that spans the area of a township, provides high-bandwidth communication over moderately inexpensive media (generally an installed CATV system using coaxial cable), may provide a switching capability, and is usually provided to all users for a subscription fee by a cable television company or a common carrier.
microprocessor	A computer whose central processing unit, and perhaps some memory, is implemented in a single integrated circuit.
microsecond	One-millionth of a second.
midsplit	A method of allocating the available bandwidth in a single-cable broadband system. Transmissions from the *headend* to the users are in the frequency range 168–300 MHz; transmissions from the users to the headend are in the frequency range 5–116 MHz.
millisecond	One-thousandth of a second.
modem	An acronym made from the words *modulator* and *demodulator*. A device that uses digital data to alter a signal that can be transmitted over an analog transmission facility (modulator) and can also receive an altered signal from an analog transmission facility and determine what digital data the alterations in the received signal represent (demodulator).
MTTR	Mean time to repair, the average amount of time it takes service personnel, after they have arrived at the site, to put a failed device into full and proper operation.
multiway comparator	An electrical circuit that can simultaneously compare one combination of bits with several other combinations of bits and determine whether that one combination of bits is equal to any of the others. Used in address recognition logic to determine whether a received message is intended for this station when this station is supposed to respond to several addresses.
multicast	A message intended for a subset of the stations on a network, rather than for an individual station or for all stations.
multiplexing	The process of sending several signals over a single transmission medium and separating them at the other end.
nanosecond	One-billionth of a second.
native mode	The use of a protocol on the type of network for which that particular protocol was developed or optimized.

NBS   National Bureau of Standards.

NCP   Network Control Protocol, the first transport level protocol used on ARPANET, superseded by *TCP*.

network access control   Electronic circuitry that determines which station may transmit next or when a particluar station may transmit. This circuitry may be centrally located or may be located in each of the *network interface controllers*.

network interface controllers   Electronic circuitry that connects a station to a network. The circuitry determines when the station may transmit, detects arriving messages, indicates error conditions, and may include buffers for storing transmitted and received messages.

network layer   The third layer in the *ISO layered model* of communications protocols. It receives data that have been framed by the data link layer below it, performs additional services, and passes the result up to the *transport layer* above it.

network relay   Another name for *router*.

network topology   The pattern of connection between points in a network. Examples include a mesh (all points connected to all other points), a *star*, a *bus*, or a *ring*.

nodes   Points in a network where service is provided, service is used, or communications channels are interconnected.

off-hook   In telephony, the state of a station requesting service from a switching system, or the state of a station that has been connected to another station and desires to maintain that connection.

open circuit   An arrangement of electrical components and wiring through which no current can flow because the wiring is disconnected at some point or because an electrical component has failed so that no current can flow.

optical fibers   See *fiber optics*.

packet   A group of bits, including data and control elements, that are switched and transmitted together. The control elements include a source address and a destination address. The data and control elements, and possibly error-control information, are arranged in a specified format.

packet buffer   Memory space set aside for storing a packet awaiting transmission or for storing a received packet. The memory may be located in the *network interface controller* or in the computer to which the controller is connected.

packet switching   A data transmission method, utilizing packets, whereby a channel is occupied only for the duration of transmission of the packet. By limiting the length of the packets, the system limits the amount of time that other users will have to wait. Depending upon the length of the message and the system being used, the data may be formatted into a packet or divided and then formatted into a number of packets for transmission and multiplexing purposes. Contrast with *circuit switching*.

parity	The number of 1s in a character or other group of bits. The number may be odd or even. If desired, a 0 or 1 may be added to the group of bits to guarantee that the number of bits is odd (or even). The data are then transmitted and the number of 1s is checked at the receiving station to see that it is still odd (or even). If it is not as expected, one knows that an error occurred. Unfortunately, the occurrence of multiple errors cannot be accurately detected.
PABX	Private automatic branch exchange. See *PBX*.
PBX	Private branch exchange, a telephone switching system that serves one company (usually), is located on the company's premises, and connects to the national telephone network.
penetration tap	A device used in Ethernet to connect a transceiver to the bus without requiring that the bus be interrupted for the installation of fittings. This is accomplished by a needlelike device that penetrates the insulation on the bus (a coaxial cable) and reaches the center conductor of the coax.
personal computer	A computer (including such elements as a keyboard, display, memory, and computational elements) provided for the use of one person and remaining idle when that person is not using it.
physical address	A grouping of numbers that identifies a particular piece of computer hardware connected to a local area network or other data communications system. Contrast with *logical address*.
physical level	The bottommost layer of the *ISO layered model* of protocols. The physical layer involves the electrical process of getting data from one point to another.
physical level relay	See *repeater*.
point-to-point	A transmission facility that connects only two points. This is in contrast to a multipoint or multidrop facility, which provides service to many points that share access to the same transmission facility.
polling	A method of controlling access to a multidrop communications facility by sending messages, addressed to each station sharing access to the facility, inquiring whether that station has any data to transmit.
preamble	A sequence of bits sent at the beginning of a transmission to condition the logic at the receiving station. The sequence does not contain message information, but rather performs transmission/reception functions such as establishing clock synchronism between the transmitting and receiving stations.
presentation level	The sixth level of the *ISO layered model* of protocols. The sixth level and those below it perform services for the top level, the application level.
preventive maintenance	The process of making repairs, adjustments, or other service to a properly functioning device with the aim of preventing it from failing.

primary buffer In a data communications device, a section of memory set aside for the transmission or reception of data. When that section of memory is empty (transmission) or full (reception), data transmission over a communications line continues using the "alternate buffer," while the associated computer transfers data to or from the primary buffer in anticipation of its use when the alternate buffer is empty or full.

printer server In a local area network, a program, residing in a computer associated with a printing device, that provides network users with shared access to the printer.

programmed i/o A method of connecting input/output devices such as terminals, card readers, and bar code readers to a computer. In this method, the arrival of data is signaled to the computer by a request for a program interrupt. During that interrupt, when it is granted, the program moves the data from the input/output device controller to computer memory. Contrast with *DMA*.

propagation velocity The speed at which an electrical (or optical) signal travels through a transmission medium.

protocol A set of rules for communicating.

protocol layers A way of thinking about communications protocols that models them as a hierarchical family in which each protocol obtains services from protocols beneath it and performs a service for protocols above it. The divisions of the hierarchy are referred to as layers or levels.

quad A type of wire used for telephone wiring in which four insulated conductors, bundled together without twisting, are encased in an overall sheath for convenience in handling. Contrast with *twisted pair*.

quantization error In the process of converting an analog signal into digital data, the difference between the signal level as expressed by the digital value and the actual analog value. Since an analog signal can have an infinite number of values, it cannot be expressed absolutely accurately without an infinite number of bits. Since that is impractical, some roundoff error must occur in choosing the digital value nearest the actual analog value.

radial wiring Wiring in which all wire runs from a common point to the point requiring service by the most direct means possible.

random retry In *Ethernet*, a station desiring to transmit and encountering a *collision* will wait a random period of time before attempting to transmit again using *CSMA/CD* rules.

rebooting The process of repeating a *booting* operation.

receiver clock circuitry Electronic components that determine where one received bit ends and another begins, and thus can generate a signal ("clock") that tells data handling logic when to record the state of a received data bit.

reconfiguration A change in the quantity, types, or arrangement of the equipment connected to a computer system. In addition to the hardware being modified, the software must be informed of the new hardware arrangement. Also, a change in the arrangement of connections in a network.

redundant circuits   Two circuits designed to perform the same task: one is used to perform the task, and the other stands by to take over performance of the task should the first one fail.

regenerating a system   Preparing the software on a computer system by telling it what the hardware configuration is and what tasks are to be performed.

relay   An electromechanical device consisting of an electromagnet whose magnetic field operates a set of contacts that establish and interrupt electrical circuits. Also, an electronic system that receives data and passes them on.

reliability   A measure of how dependably a system performs once a person is actually using the system. Contrast with *availability*.

remote log-in   The ability to *log in* to the computer system that one normally uses, although one is currently using a terminal connected to another computer system.

repeater   A device used at the physical level of the *ISO layered model* of communications protocols that amplifies or otherwise conditions signals received from one piece of a transmission medium and passes them on to another, similar piece of transmission medium without reading or altering the addresses or the data content. Also called a level 1 relay or a physical level relay.

retransmission   A method of error control in which stations receiving messages acknowledge the receipt of correct messages and either do not acknowledge or acknowledge in the negative for the receipt of incorrect messages. The lack of acknowledgment or receipt of negative acknowledgment is an indication to the sending station that it should transmit the failed message again. Retransmission is preferable to methods that repair a few damaged bits by sending special codes, because typical communications lines have bursts of errors that severely damage an occasional message rather than slightly damage many messages.

ring   A local area network topology in which each station is connected to two other stations, this process being repeated until a loop is formed. Data are transmitted from station to station around the loop, always in the same direction.

ring buffers   A method of storing data in memory such that the same locations in memory are being continually reused. A "write pointer" specifies where new data are to be written, and a "read pointer" specifies the next location to be read. When all locations have been read or written, the process resumes ("wraps around") and starts at the beginning of the block of memory being used. Obviously, the write pointer must not be allowed to write over data not yet read, and the read pointer must not point to locations not rewritten since the last read. This system is also used with *linked list headers* arranged as ring buffers, in which case the write and read pointers complement a single bit in the header indicating whether the data buffer pointed to by the header has been read or written.

ROM   Acronym for read-only memory, a data storage device that cannot be written by normal computer circuitry, but rather must be programmed by special circuitry, generally using higher voltages and currents than those within the computer. Such devices have the advantage of not being changed by malfunctions within the computer that might cause changes in the contents of normal types of memory. Thus, they are often used for storing programs used in *booting*.

round-trip delay   See *round-trip time*.

round-trip time   The amount of time it takes an electrical signal to travel from one end of a transmission medium to the other and back. This is important in *CSMA/CD* systems because a station at one end of the transmission medium cannot be sure it has begun a collision-free transmission until the signal has reached the far end, and possibly collided with a transmission just beginning there, and the collision condition has returned to this station.

routers   In a local area network, a device that receives physical-level signaling from a network, performs data-link-level and network-level protocol processes upon those signals, and then sends them via appropriate data-link-level and physical-level protocols onto another network. The transport, session, presentation, and application levels of the information handled remain unchanged. As the name implies, the primary function of a router is to determine how to forward a packet toward its destination, based on tables within the router that indicate the costs, congestion status, and other factors associated with possible routes. Also called a level 3 relay or an intermediate system.

routing   The process of determining how to forward a packet toward its destination, based on tables that indicate the costs, congestion status, and other factors associated with possible routes.

routing tables   Tables that indicate the costs, congestion status, and other factors associated with possible routes.

SDLC   Synchronous Data Link Control, an IBM data link layer protocol in which data are transmitted with a 0 inserted after each consecutive group of five 1s, except for a distinctive flag pattern (01111110), which delineates the beginning and end of a frame. This protocol is very similar to *HDLC*, but the header limits the addressing and message numbering to fewer bits.

segments   In a local area network utilizing a bus topology, electrically continuous pieces of bus, made of the same transmission media. Segments may be connected to each other via *repeaters*.

serial interface   The "lowest common denominator" of data communications; the simplest possible mechanism for converting the parallel arrangement of bits used within computers to the serial (one bit after the other) form used on data transmission lines and vice versa. At least one is generally provided on all computers for the connection of a terminal.

server
: A program, and possibly a dedicated computer system, that provides a service to local area network users, such as shared access to a file system, control of a printer, or the storage of messages in a mail system.

session level
: The fifth level in the *ISO layered model*. The session level receives the services of protocols located in the transport level and below, and performs services for the presentation and application levels above it.

shadowing
: The process of maintaining a duplicate of the file and making modifications to that file in step with the modifications being made by the user to the main version of the file.

shielding
: The process of enclosing a wire or circuit with a grounded metallic structure, so that electrical signals outside the structure cannot reach the wire, and so that signals on the wire cannot reach beyond the structure, except to the apparatus to which the wire connects.

short circuit
: An electrical system in which current flows directly from one conductor to the other without passing through the device(s) that is supposed to receive the current. This condition is generally caused by the electrical conductors' being in accidental contact with each other at some point between the power source and the device that is supposed to receive the power.

signal conditioning
: The amplification or modification of electrical signals to make them more appropriate for transmission over a particular medium.

signal conversion device
: An electrical circuit that changes electrical signals from one form to another. For example, from *TTL* levels to light for transmission through a *fiber optics* system.

signal relections
: A condition that arises when an electrical signal passing through a transmission medium, such as a *bus*, encounters a point where the *impedance* changes. Part of the electrical signal will continue ahead, while part of the signal will return (reflect) back toward its origin. If there are several impedance discontinuities nearby, portions of the signal may reflect at several points, and the reflected signals may reinforce each other as they return toward the source, causing devices attached to the bus to have difficulty receiving the correct signal information.

signal level
: The strength of a signal, generally expressed in either absolute units of voltage or power, or in units relative to the strength of the signal at its source.

simplex
: A system in which transmission can take place only in one direction.

Slotted ALOHA
: A method of accessing a computer network in which a station desiring to transmit does so without listening for other stations to be silent, without waiting for permission, but rather whenever it pleases, subject only to the constraint that it must await a time tick. The "transmit at will" system of accessing

a transmission medium is referred to as an *ALOHA* system, but the addition of the time-tick constraint creates a slotted ALOHA system, which has roughly twice the throughput.

SNA Systems Network Architecture, IBM's layered communications protocols.

software Programs stored in easily alterable form, such as in computer memory, on disks, or on tapes. Contrast with *firmware* and *hardware*.

source address That part of a message which indicates from whom the message originated.

space division switch In telephone switching, a system in which each conversation takes a physically identifiable path that is not shared by any other conversation. Contrast with *time division switching*.

spine network In local area networks, a network to which users' computers and network servers do not connect directly. Instead, users' computers and network servers connect to *access networks*, and the access networks are connected via *gateways* to the spine, thus providing interconnection of the access networks.

splitters In broadband systems, devices that allow branches to be connected to the cable system.

standards Documents that describe an agreed-upon way of doing things such that independent groups or companies can design and build hardware, firmware, software, or combinations thereof and have them interwork with similar products designed and built by others.

star A local area network topology in which all stations are wired to a central station that establishes, maintains, and breaks connections between the stations. Also descriptive of wiring patterns in which *radial wiring* is used, although the control of connections is established in some other fashion.

station Equipment, such as a computer or terminal, attached to a local area network and used to provide services to network users, or used to provide a person with computational services and/or access to the network.

station address A grouping of numbers that uniquely identifies a *station* in a local area network. Data transmitted from the station will bear this grouping of numbers as a *source address*, and data destined for this station will bear this grouping of numbers as a *destination address*.

store and forward A method of switching messages in which a message from one station is received at a computer acting as a switch and is stored there. After the computer has determined the destination address (a method of sending the message to that destination) and an available communications circuit, the message is forwarded on its way toward the destination. This method is also called message switching. *Packet switching* is a special case of store-and-forward switching in which the length of transmissions handled is limited by breaking up long messages into packets.

stub	In local area networks utilizing buses, any electrical connection to the bus, especially one that does not have the same *impedance* as the bus. Such connections create *signal reflections* whose magnitude depends upon the length of the wire used in the connection and the difference between the impedance of the connecting wire and the impedance of the bus.
subsplit	A method of allocating the available bandwidth in a single-cable broadband system. Transmissions from the *headend* to the users are in the frequency range 54–300 MHz; transmissions from the users to the headend are in the frequency range 5–32 MHz.
switch module	In a distributed *PBX*, a unit of electronic circuitry to which some modest number of stations, such as 64, 128, or 256, connect. Calls between the attached stations may be handled within the unit. Calls to other stations, or calls requiring access to network services, pass from unit to unit over some type of local area network.
system console	A terminal devoted to controlling a computer system rather than a terminal intended for use in obtaining computational services. The terminal may have more switches and indicators than a conventional terminal and may have the capability of invoking actions, such as *booting*, that conventional terminals cannot invoke.
T1 carrier	A time-division-multiplex transmission system introduced by the Bell System in 1962. Eight thousand times per second, an 8-bit sample from each of 24 voice channels is transmitted, along with a framing bit whose binary sense varies in a prescribed fashion. The transmission of 193 bits 8,000 times per second produces a 1.544-megabit transmission rate.
tap	In a local area network, an electrical connection permitting signals to be transmitted onto or received from a bus.
TCP	Transmission Control Protocol, the transport level protocol used on ARPANET.
TCP/IP	Transmission Control Protocol/Internet Protocol, the combination of transport and network level protocols adopted for networkwide use on the ARPANET on 1 January 1983.
terminal	An input/output device consisting of at least a keyboard and a display (paper or video), intended for human interaction with a computer. A "dumb terminal" consists only of the parts mentioned above, while a "smart terminal" contains some computer functions such as editing and message formatting.
terminal concentrator	A device that connects several (approximately 4 to 40) terminals to a local area network. It takes characters typed, or lines of text, or entire screens of text, and formats them into a form suitable for transmission over the network.
terminal multiplexer	A device that takes typed character streams from several terminals and transfers them through a common transmission medium (sometimes shared with other users) to a distant point where separate character streams appropriate to each terminal are again formed.

terminator
An electrical device that can be attached to the end of a cable to simulate the attachment of an indefinite amount of additional cable. If this device has the same *impedance* as the cable, signals arriving at the end of the cable and encountering this device will not experience an *impedance discontinuity*, and *signal reflections* will not be created.

terminated drop
Wiring intended for use by a single user whose equipment has not yet been installed. In place of the equipment, a *terminator* has been installed so that the network electrical characteristics will be the same as if the correct equipment were in place.

throughput
The amount of work performed by a computer, or the amount of data passed through a network, per unit time or as a percentage of the time available.

time division multiplexing
A method of sharing a transmission facility among many users by allocating short periods of time for each pair of transmitting and receiving stations to use the facility.

time division switching
A method of switching data or voice that has been encoded (see *encoding*) into the form of data. There are buses within the switch that are shared by *time division multiplexing*. Logic circuits sample data from one bus, store it, and deposit it on another bus to achieve the switching function.

time domain reflectometer (TDR)
A piece of test apparatus that places a pulse of electrical energy on a cable and then connects the cable to a display upon which an electron beam is moving from left to right as a function of elapsed time. If the cable contains an *impedance discontinuity*, there will be a *signal reflection* and a portion of the transmitted electrical pulse will return to the TDR and be displayed as a deflection of the electron beam on the display. By measuring the position of the beam deflection on the display and thus determining the time at which it occurred, one can determine the location of the impedance discontinuity, which indicates a cable fault.

timesharing
A method of allowing many people to use a computer simultaneously by dividing its available time into slices, each devoted to a particular user's task. If time slices occur frequently enough, each user thinks he or she has sole use of the computer. All of the users have shared access to services such as a printer, a file system, and mail. It is the role of servers in a local area network to provide these services for users of *personal computers*.

token
In a local area network, a unique combination of bits, receipt of which indicates permission to transmit.

token bus
The use of a *token* to control access to a bus. A station receiving the token transmits if desired and then forwards the token to a specified next address.

token ring
The use of a *token* to control access to a ring. A station receives all messages currently circulating on the ring, followed by the token. The station may allow everything to pass (copying messages addressed to it and removing any mes-

sages it sent) and append a message to those circulating and then reinsert the token.

transceiver	A device that uses digital data to create a signal that can be transmitted over a substantial distance (several kilometers) and can receive such signals and determine what digital data were used to create them. Transceivers differ from long line drivers, as transceivers are bidirectional, often convey clocking information within the data, and are designed for greater speeds and distances. Transceivers differ from modems, as transceivers need not modulate a carrier to perform their task.
transmission media	Anything, such as wire, *coaxial cable*, *fiber optics*, air, or vacuum, that is being used to propagate an electrical signal and thus is propagating electrically represented information.
transport level	The fourth level in the *ISO layered model*. The transport level receives the services of protocols located in the network level and below, and performs services for the session, presentation, and application levels above it.
TTL	Transistor transistor logic, descriptive of the electronic circuits used in typical computers.
twisted pair	Two insulated wires wrapped one about the other in a uniform fashion so that each is equally exposed to electrical signals impinging upon the wires from their environment. The pair of wires may be surrounded by a shield, a jacket of additional insulation, or similar pairs of wires.
vendor code	Software written by the same company that manufactured the computer system on which it is running (or not running . . .).
virtual circuit	A system that delivers *packets* in guaranteed sequential order, just as they would arrive over a real *point-to-point* electrical circuit.
VLSI	Very large scale integration, the art of putting hundreds of thousands of transistors into a single integrated circuit, typically a quarter-inch square.
voice annotated text	A system in which a message can be delivered to a user's terminal and displayed upon a screen with certain portions marked in a distinctive way. When the user directs a pointer of some type to the marked section, voice commentary is delivered through a speaker or telephone handset associated with the terminal.
voltage	A measure of electrical potential, expressed in units of volts, named after Count Alessandro Volta.
volt-ohm-meter (VOM)	A piece of test apparatus that measures and displays voltage, resistance, and current. Such devices are quite inexpensive and are the most basic piece of electrical test apparatus available.
watchdog timer	A circuit or program that periodically generates a signal that must be acknowledged by the program performing the major functions in the associated computer system. If the acknowledgment does not occur within a prescribed pe-

riod of time, the main program or computer system will be deemed to have failed, and an alarm will be sounded or a backup computer system will take over.

waveform The pattern made on a piece of paper or other display when the voltage of a signal is plotted as a function of time.

Winchester disk An economical, high-density magnetic storage system pioneered by IBM for use in its 3030 disk system. The number 3030 also being a famous model of rifle made by the Winchester Arms Company, the nickname Winchester was applied to the disk.

windows A method of displaying information on a screen in which the viewer sees what appear to be several sheets of paper much as they would appear on a desktop. The viewer can shift the positions of the sheets on the screen. The system is particularly attractive for working on several related tasks, or portions of the same task, simultaneously.

wire centers Token ring networks may use *radial wiring* plans rather than running wires in an actual circle. When such systems use radial wiring, two pairs of wires (transmit and receive) run from a central point to each station like spokes of wheels radiating from hubs. The central points or hubs are the wire centers, points at which the transmit pair from one station is connected to the receive pair from the next in a consecutive fashion until an electrical ring has been formed.

word processing The use of a computer, especially a *personal computer*, to assist in composing, editing, formatting, and printing memorandums, letters, books, or other text material.

XNS Xerox Network Services, Xerox Corporation's layered data communications protocols.

Index